DIVORCE SUCKS

what to do when irreconcilable
differences, lawyer fees, and your ex's
Hollywood Wife make you miserable

MARY JO EUSTACE

EDITED BY JOANNE KIMES,
SUCKS SERIES CREATOR

Adams Media
New York London Toronto Sydney New Delhi

adamsmedia

Adams Media
An Imprint of Simon & Schuster, Inc.
57 Littlefield Street
Avon, Massachusetts 02322

For information about special discounts for bulk purchases, please contact Simon & Schuster Special Sales at 1-866-506-1949 or business@simonandschuster.com.

The Simon & Schuster Speakers Bureau can bring authors to your live event. For more information or to book an event contact the Simon & Schuster Speakers Bureau at 1-866-248-3049 or visit our website at www.simonspeakers.com.

Manufactured in the United States of America

Library of Congress Cataloging-in-Publication Data has been applied for.

POD ISBN 978-1-4405-6350-8

dedication

This is book is dedicated to my holy trinity:

To my son Jack, my wonderful little mini-me who makes me laugh harder than anyone.

My beautiful daughter Lola, a celestial angel from another place and time.

And finally to my greatest source of inspiration and strength, my spectacular mother, Maureen.

Without the three of you, everyday would be Tuesday . . .

acknowledgments

I would like to thank and acknowledge the many people who came aboard my divorce cruise and never jumped ship even when the waters were rough and turbulent.

Meredith O'Hayre and Joanne Kimes for their editorial and emotional support and not hating me when I preferred my edits over theirs.

My fantastic arsenal of priceless friends who let me go on and on about my divorce and never once fell asleep or yelled at me for being boring and self-indulgent.

I would like to give a shout out to Ken Kostick, my evil twin.

Anne Fenn and Sally Tindal, the most fantastic women ever.

Risa Gertner, for always making me feel at home and doing everything possible to help me stay in California.

Barbara Bardee and Linda Stregger, for employing me and helping me buy my first house as a single lady.

For Aunt Sue for all her help and prayers (especially in trying to find me a boyfriend).

For all the horrible things that people and tabloids and cyberspace said about me—from being old and ugly to verging on lunacy—thank you. I could have not become the woman I am without your help.

And finally to all you women out there divorcing or divorced and getting through—here's to you:

To your new life, your tremendous courage, and your best adventure yet . . . your life.

MJ

contents

divorce sucks—all the time

Please allow me to introduce myself. My name is Mary Jo Eustace and I'm divorced. I have two children, so I guess technically speaking, I'm a single mother, even though that label still catches me off guard. I'm forty-six years old, although many tabloids peg me at sixty-two (but more of that fun stuff later).

I'm just a nice girl from Canada who came to California with my then six-year-old son and my seemingly adoring husband to fulfill his childhood dream of becoming a big, huge American star. We packed up our lives and relocated to Los Angeles—leaving our house, friends, families, and careers (mine at least) behind. We moved into a *Leave It to Beaver* neighborhood, complete with white picket fences and oranges that spilled off the trees while kids played on the streets all year round. We marched in the Halloween parade and celebrated the Fourth of July with enormous pride and my world famous teriyaki burgers.

And just as we started to settle into our own little version of a Norman Rockwell painting, another bolt of good fortune came our way. We were chosen by a birth mother to be the adoptive parents of her darling little girl, my beautiful (now three-year-old) daughter, Lola. After years of failed fertility treatments and adoption home studies we were now parents again almost seven years after having our son, Jack. Seriously, not to be smug, but at this point, I thought we had it really going on. Plus on top of all that amazing good fortune, my husband finally got an acting gig on a Lifetime movie—talk about an aphrodisiac! It's funny as I write about this now. I can still remember sitting in our California cottage, holding my newborn daughter in my arms, thinking to myself, "Life can't possibly get any better than this." What I failed to factor in was that it could sure get a hell of a lot worse.

So in the spirit of the whole Hollywood theme, let's cut to seven weeks later, shall we? Once again, I'm holding my daughter in my arms, but this time I'm on vacation and in a Palm Springs hotel room and not our cozy little house. My husband is there (anyway, I think it is him) and he's telling me he's leaving me for a Hollywood actress. I ask when and he says "right now." He tells me that money will never be a problem and that he has met his soul mate. He then rents a car and proceeds to leave. I start to take note of his obvious absence and begin to realize that perhaps I'm in store for a completely different type of trip, one that I will refer to many times in this book. I call it the all-you-can-suffer, guaranteed-to-make-you-sick-and-slightly-crazy, "Divorce Cruise."

After he left I stayed up all night looking at the desert sky, racking my brains for solutions or signs or an imploding star to help guide me through this very real nightmare that I was about to enter. I was so naive—I really had no idea what was to come or where to start. This divorce that was about to take over my life was something that I knew nothing about. The only thing I did know was that it totally and completely sucked and it was not supposed to happen to me. Yet even in my pain and suffering and complete devastation, I did smell a substantial weight loss coming on. Thank God I was right about something.

Cut back to real time and where I am at this very moment. I am stronger, smarter, nicer, and in many ways even happier. I also think I look better—or maybe I just look more like myself. Let's face it. If we can't learn something from the implosion of our entire world, then what the hell is the point anyway?

Let The Games Begin ...

Of course, nobody ever thinks they will end up getting divorced, but if you're reading this book, it appears you may have entered the 51 percent club—named for the percentage of marriages that end in a split.

Divorce is the modern plague of our time. From the humiliation of your family being public fodder, to slimy divorce lawyers (sorry legal profession, but you do need to be revamped), to seeing your ex-husband three weeks out engaged to your former best friend—divorce is an experience like no other, and in its wake, many a good women has been pulled under.

But isn't it time to rewrite that story? No doubt about it, divorce is a horrendous life-altering experience that will pull you down before it spits you out. But make no mistake. It is not a death sentence! As a matter of fact, it can be one of the most life affirming things you will ever go through—if you let it. We as women have to share our stories for so many reasons: to commiserate, to heal, and believe it or not, to laugh. And if you stick with me through this book, I promise you will laugh more than once, and maybe even out loud.

Even though it was a hard decision, I decided to share my stories with you because I feel I have learned so much through this experience, and if recounting some of my own personal horrors can be of help to others, then I am game. From the lovely way I found out about my impending divorce, to assembling my legal and psychological teams, to learning how to laugh and live again, I believe we all have to keep talking to keep thriving.

Before I was divorced, if someone had dared to predict my roller coaster ride of emotional turmoil, I don't know if I could have withstood it. But sometimes stumbling into the unknown with just your adrenaline is a good thing. For a while, that will get you by. But there will come a time when you need to be at the top of your game as you systematically rebuild the pieces of your life into the type of structure you want to reside within. It's all about the second act, baby, and this is your opportunity to make it the best act ever!

Together we will go through the breakup; the residual anger and emotional devastation; money, sex, legal, spiritual, physiological warfare; personal hygiene; male escorts and endorphins—and that's just Chapter 1 (buh dum bum)! From how you found out about your own personal divorce cruise, to fighting for your kids and your financial rights, we will navigate the waters of modern-day divorce with an arsenal of solid information aimed at getting you through.

We will tell our stories, the good, the bad, and the truly ugly, and come to own our experiences, rather than pretending the whole thing never happened.

It's through accepting responsibility for ourselves and our lives that we will redefine the image of the "sad and lonely divorced woman" forever. It's also worth noting that the final chapter of this book is about remarriage. So even though it all seems a little daunting now, there is a whole lot of hope happening when we are done.

We all have our own stories, idealized or not, about our marriages. But faster than Angelina Jolie can adopt another baby, we can become that couple, that marriage that people have known for months was "on the rocks." As women we are no longer a part of a couple, but rather the "sad single mother" or the "broken older woman" who stupidly supported her husband through dental school while he was applying veneers for free, if you know what I mean. We become an instant statistic, a completely different version of ourselves as we cross the great divide between being married and single. All of a sudden we belong to a whole new club—and it's a club that has no facilities, indoor plumbing, or healthy snacks. Plus all the other members are really cranky. So before we start on our journey to wellness, let's talk. How did this whole thing get kicked off for you? I bet everyone has a different version to tell. . . .

chapter 1

i don't

This is how I found out I was getting divorced. My husband, Dean, had been away for three weeks making a movie in our country of origin, Canada, when he returned to Los Angeles with some very surprising news. He was having an affair with his costar, Tori Spelling, and he would be leaving me for her rather immediately. She was married as well, although briefly, but that did not seem to be an issue. We were also in the process of adopting Lola who was seven weeks old at the time but again, that did not seem to be an issue. As a matter of fact, Dean signed off on her adoption a week later. As mentioned, we were on vacation in Palm Springs with another couple (lucky them), so after he left I had a lot of explaining to do down at the pool. At this point, I was hoping for a natural disaster to put me out of my misery, but no such luck. As a matter of fact, I was so guilt ridden with what was in store for my family that

I took my son for a seven-hour play date at the nearest McDonald's. How's that for parenting 101?

Once the dust settled, oh let's say, a whole week later, at approximately 3:14 P.M. PST on a Monday afternoon, I was doing homework with my son, feeling a little scared that third-grade math seemed to be significantly beyond my comfort zone, when the doorbell rang. I was being served divorce papers. At the same moment, my neighbor was coming to my door as well. Ironically, this neighbor is an actor and played Dr. Mancini on *Melrose Place*, a Spelling Production no less. Seems he had somehow forgotten that my husband had just left me. As the papers were being served, he asked when Dean was coming home because he needed to borrow something I didn't even know we owned. I reminded him that Dean had left and that's why I was now being served divorce papers. He looked a little confused and then embarrassed and never brought it up again. A year later, he would be served with his own divorce papers. As would another couple just two doors down. Three divorces in one year. All in all, a very bad year for Ben Avenue.

Mine is just one story. There are certainly other permutations of how the divorce deals go down. High up on the pain threshold ladder is the devastating one-two punch with a blindsiding thrown in for good measure. This is where your best friend stops by for an unexpected visit and admits she's been having a three-year affair with your gnarly-ass husband. While you're attempting to process this and wondering whom you hate more, her or your husband, the blindsiding comes in: "And we'll both be filing for divorce." So what we have here is your basic double betrayal: a blindsiding and an avoidance advantage for your husband as he completely compartmentalizes and denies you any human qualities.

Now I know this one sounds bad and I put it in the category of nanny, secretary, or next-door neighbor, but it can get worse. Just replace "best friend" with "sibling" (perhaps your hotter, younger sister) and proceed to seek professional help—right now!

The blindsiding scenario is pretty much the worst because it really comes out of nowhere, with absolutely no warning. And it would make sense that the surprise nature of this announcement usually involves a party leaving for another party, typically with the husband dumping his wife for a younger, more user-friendly, version. There's almost nothing you can do to see it coming, after all (and this is really important), people only show you what they want you to see. So now is not the time to beat yourself up because you think you missed some crucial piece of information that would have saved your marriage. Chances are, your best friend was probably not a really good friend, but we will address that later. For now it is sufficient to just hate her guts.

Of course, there are other vignettes. Perhaps it was a mutual decision to end the marriage and there are no third parties involved. Seems rather adult, right? Both participants recognizing the twilight nature of the relationship and letting go mutually and respectfully, dividing the children and assets fairly and without rancor or emotions. Seems like a perfect scenario (and the basis for a television sitcom), but in reality, things seldom go like that. Just ask any family lawyer and she will tell you that a murder trial has more levity and humanity then a typical divorce case. I guess the old adage "You can hate as much as you can love" is true. Even if you both got to the decision together, there are miles to go before you sleep.

No matter how you arrived at this divorce juncture, count on taking a lot of baggage with you. After all, this was your family, for God's sake. I've talked to plenty of people who left and acquiesced on everything for peace, and guess what? It was still hell! Sometimes it's not about the things or even the children. It's actually about the death of your relationship. Sorry to get serious here, but when we got married, we took our dreams and our faith and made a big bold statement to the world: "I am so sure of my judgment and my ability to trust that I am going to create my very own oasis, a testament to my belief in family, love, and commitment." And when that unit as we know it comes undone, it unravels to the bone, leaving us no choice but to question everything.

Okay, I am a little tired after that last paragraph, because, let's face it: this shit is hard. But understanding why we are so hurt can help us take care of ourselves and our children in a much better way. And getting to understanding takes talking. So, as I will continue to recommend throughout the book, if you have any divorced or divorcing friends, get together and start sharing stories. Yes, you will cry, but you'll also laugh your ass off. Believe it or not, divorce can be funny. Especially when you share your stories with a group of women. Oprah is really big on the idea that everybody has an important story and they should all be shared. And the more stories you hear, the less alone you will feel. And that, my friend, will start to make you feel better.

How the Divorce Can Go Down

With more than 50 percent of all marriages ending in divorce, did we go into this union with archaic ideas about the real longevity of the institution? Did we set ourselves up for failure by not really understanding the meaning of "Til death do us part?" Well, when you think about it, having the word death in any vow is a bit creepy to begin with, but I wonder if we get so caught up in the actual wedding that we forget the marriage itself isn't just an afterthought. It's socially unifying to plan your wedding and broadcast your love to the world. But when the day is over, you're just two people living together, day to day, trying to figure out when the fun starts. To coin a phrase, marriage is a marathon not for the faint of heart. And if I think back to the days before I said "I do," I have to admit that this crossed my mind countless times before, during, and after my wedding day.

It's Amazing Any Marriage Survives

I'm sure you've heard all sorts of reasons why marriages fail: money, sex, children, work, diet, video games, natural disasters, addictions, and escalating gas prices. When you think of it, with the endless laundry list of negatives, how do any survive at all? If you take a close look at the list, aren't all these variables just components of everyday life? Statistics back this up. They claim that 43 percent of all first marriages end in divorce, 60 percent of second marriages the same way, and if you think third time is a charm, think again. That divorce rate is 73 percent. Now, I am not a forensic scientist, but it appears that we're not getting this thing right. I would have thought that childless couples had the hometown advantage (no kids mean less irritation, fewer financial obligations, and so on), but apparently their divorce rate is only slightly lower. So if you're feeling badly about your divorce glitch, think of it this way: it was sort of a head or tails situation anyway.

> **"I knew we were in trouble when**
>
> **I asked my husband what he wanted**
>
> **for dinner and he said a divorce. Usually**
>
> **he just wants chicken, not separate lives."**
>
> ~Donna

What Went Horribly Wrong

Pinpointing the straw that broke the camels back might actually be helpful. I remember sitting on my front porch a few months before my husband left, thinking, "I really don't want to be married anymore." For some reason, the thought of the whole "'til death do us part" thing was causing me great distress and I didn't know why. I was beginning to wonder if a lifetime with one person was really achievable without a partial lobotomy or dabbling in some sort of extracurricular activities (which, by the way, women are doing at an alarming rate). It seems that the old institution of marriage in its present format just is not cutting it. It makes you wonder: what are we all really looking for? And furthermore, if women keep getting more and more self-sufficient, how much will they be willing to give up to get and stay married? It's a good question—find a water cooler and discuss.

But I digress. For me it probably wasn't a good sign that the sight of him in the morning, wearing his ill-fitted white waffle robe, slurping his black coffee, and lecturing me on proper refrigerator etiquette caused my mind to wander. Did you know that one of the top ten things wives fantasize about is killing their husbands? I guess it would make sense that men might be thinking the same thing. Isn't that lovely though—co-planning each other's demise while stirring in your coffee creamer? The thing of dreams, baby!

I've heard the two biggest deal breakers for marriage are money and sex. I am not sure which one comes first but if I had to hazard a guess, I would think that it would be sex. Of course, sex is about power, too, but more than that, it really is the emotional watershed of your relationship. According to Dr. Phil (and I have seen him yell at many women about this), sex is the way men express themselves to their partners, while women use sex to achieve the intimacy they crave. Sure, there are times we just want a good bang, but according to statistics, a husband loading up the dishwasher is the greatest foreplay a woman will ever experience (this being referred to as "choreplay"). So when the sex starts to go in a marriage, men lose their number one form of expression, and women, exhausted and tired of being mauled by the kids and their husbands, are secretly relieved. I have had many discussions with women about this subject and found that when they are just too overwhelmed and sometimes resentful of their husband's lack of involvement around the home, they completely say goodbye to their sex life.

Chances are if the thought of sex with your husband causes you to go to bed at 7:30 and fake sleep apnea on a frequent basis, there could be some other issues in your marriage. Plus, if he starts working out, working late, and not working on you, he could have his affections parked somewhere else. The demise of your sex life or a significant change in quantity is usually a big fat red flag that there are problems ahead. You may wake up one day and no longer recognize yourself or your partner. Remember that Talking Heads song "Once In a Lifetime"? You may wake up one day in a beautiful house, with a beautiful life, yet nothing makes sense. Ever felt that way? Especially lately?

Now on to the money thing. Money really is about power—for the one who has it—and freedom. In many ways, the person controlling the purse strings is the person orchestrating the relationship. Here is where some women make a most horrendous mistake: they abdicate themselves right out of the family's finances and haven't a clue to what is going on. They give up their money for the good of the family and when things start to unravel, they have no recourse or financial wherewithal to extricate themselves from their situation. In a word, they become stuck—stuck in a bad relationship and beholden to someone they can't stand who is telling them that tampons are a luxury item. You may want to have separate accounts, some source of independent revenue outside of the marriage and an understanding of basic finances so you are not left emotionally and financially bankrupt from your divorce. Even if it means rolling pennies and taking back pop bottles, start to have some fiscal responsibility now.

Signs that your marriage is failing could be anywhere. Here are but a few:

The Top Ten Signs Your Marriage Is Failing

1. You find panties in his car . . . and yours (barf).
2. He has started to spray in his bald spot.
3. His cell phone bill necessitates a line of credit.
4. He asks you to sign documents . . . in another language.
5. He starts wearing toddler clothing—i.e., baggy shorts and angry T-shirts better suited for a twenty-year-old.
6. A terminal disease feels like a tax rebate.
7. The Godfather becomes your marriage manual.
8. Hearing him breathe bugs you.
9. You start envying widows.

And the number one sign your marriage is failing . . .

10. You wish that it would.

Trying to Keep the Ship from Going Down

Assuming that your divorce papers haven't been signed, sealed, and delivered, you may find yourself at a crossroad right now. Presuming that you're unhappy in your marriage and that your husband didn't dump you via e-mail or run off with your mother (it happens), you recognize that unless you act quickly, this party is over. It's already been established that things aren't working like they should and let's face it, you're unhappy. So now you have to decide what to do about it.

Even though your world feels endless now, the longer you wait, the more your life can zip by right in front of

you. If you're planning on taking major action, be strategic—don't waste time. Plan on taking care of yourself and
your life, right now. You've acknowledged that something
is wrong—which is a huge step. Now let's see if you can fix
it. Can you save your marriage? And, probably more importantly, do you want to save your marriage?

So how can you do that? At this point, your communication with your spouse might be nonexistent, and worse still,
you might be enjoying that fact (not hearing the sound of his
condescending, seizure-inducing voice is no doubt a bit of a red
flag, but let's move on). This is the part where couples look for
that third-party intervention, otherwise known as marital therapy—a neutral observer who can guide you two back together,
stronger, better, united. Therapists can also act like a security
guard if you will, removing sharp objects from purses and
explaining why nothing says "I love you" like a switchblade.

Marriage Counselors—Paying the Ultimate Price

The first time I really became aware of marriage
counselors was when my parents went years ago when
they were having some serious marital problems. Oddly
enough, their counselor turned out to be someone I
once dated. I was tempted to call him up and warn him
about how crazy my parents can be, but I thought it
best to stay out of it. Shortly after their therapy ended,
he died. To this day, I still feel a bit responsible. Dealing with my two insane parents must have contributed
to his demise. Luckily, there was something that survived: my parent's marriage. Forty-eight years so far.

When it comes to marriage counseling, often one spouse
wants to go and the other doesn't. Or at least I find that

to be the case with most couples I know. I've even heard of therapy being used as an ultimatum and even then, one spouse still refused to go. And I must admit that was me, too. When we first moved to L.A., Dean asked me to go to a marriage counselor, but I refused. Maybe I didn't think we needed it. Boy, did I play that one wrong. Could it have saved my marriage? I don't know. But it might have made for a very different ending.

Surprisingly, statistics show that once you start marriage counseling, things may actually get worse. I mean, how could they get better? It makes sense if you think about it. The dirty little secret of a failing marriage is that you can't tell the other person what you really think—that would be cruel. It is very hard to tell the other party in your struggling relationship what you really think of him to his face and have much good come from it. Once you open that Pandora's box, can you ever really go back?

Preventative Maintenance

While we can't go back in time, the new trend in counseling is for the couple to enter therapy before they get married. This could be the ticket to a great marriage. If you're smart enough to look at the act of marriage that seriously and confess you might need some help on how to get on the good side of the fifty-fifty statistic, then counseling could be a useful tool.

Premarital counseling gives you the full scoop before you commit. It's like dying your hair blond: to enjoy the benefits, you really have to do the maintenance. And it does seem that couples who check in regularly with each other and actually monitor their relationship seem, well, happy. Seeing a therapist before walking down the aisle redefines the fantasy. It's not all about the dress and the presents—okay maybe a little bit about the presents—but about the state of the union. If you know what you're getting into before you enter on your journey through life together, odds are the final destination won't be divorce. Quite simply, you probably have a better shot of staying together. I know this idea of counseling before committing is too late for you now, but it's something to remember if you ever decide to walk down the aisle again. But I'm getting way ahead of myself.

Facing the Butt-Ugly Truth

If you're really serious about salvaging your marriage, you might have to suck it up and expose yourself to the truth about your relationship. And even though the act of wading through all your personal muck might be painful and perhaps even counterproductive, it's probably a gamble worth taking.

To find a good therapist, ask friends and family that you relate to. Find out what advice their therapist gave them so you can see if you agree. You can also talk to your primary care physician to see if he or she recommends any therapists in particular. Then, try him out and take him for a spin. Oh, and it wouldn't hurt to Google the therapist's name beforehand to see if he has any prior malpractice suits. And finally, for God's sake, make sure you're not seeing your husband's new girlfriend or someone who gets a kickback from a divorce attorney and funeral homes. This person could be the lifeline to resuscitating your gasping relationship, so it's important to do some legwork.

As unpleasant as all this is, its now time to practice what is really the mantra of this book: whatever the choice, whatever the outcome, you must take control of your life, such as it is, and make the decisions to get you where you want to be. Plan Bs are great, hell, so are Plan As, but at this point in the wake-up call of your marriage, you have to be involved in all of them.

If you can't agree on the counseling thing, what about agreeing to take a weekend getaway? A few days together with just the two of you, no kids, no BlackBerrys, no excuses. Life goes so fast and as simple as this sounds, slowing down and taking time for yourselves as a couple can be highly effective. Just starting with the basic premise of "Remember me? How are you?" might be a good start. It might give you a clearer view of what being apart would mean to each other, to the family, to your lives, and your future. You could all of a sudden see each other very differently: would you want him dating that crazy single lady from your son's school? It could really bring how you feel into focus quickly. And what about your husband? Would he want you to be taken by another man, never to be returned again?

On the flipside, if the idea of life apart would actually feel like "a get out of jail free" card, then you should proceed to the next portion of this chapter.

When to Call It Quits

It's tough to gauge when you should throw in the towel. After all, people can survive on a Triscuit for weeks after a plane crash, battle horrendous diseases and obstacles without complaint, give up kidneys for a loved one, and generally take on the world and all its ailments and not break a sweat. In comparison, really, how bad can staying in your marriage be?

That's a good question. In general, we're told to "suck it up" and that "things could always be worse," and "if life gives you lemons, make lemonade." In summary, stop your whining already and just move on. I guess that can work for things like parking tickets and being skipped over for a promotion, but your life probably deserves a little more self-examination than that. A life unexamined is a life not really lived fully. Translation: basically, you're sucking at life if you don't question your own truth and worth. We all go through patches where we're lost, but we should never stop questioning and growing and moving forward. Yes, people get married and fall asleep at the wheel—that's just standard practice as we all try to navigate the winding highway that is our lives. But when this happens, be honest about it and don't feel like a failure. The human collective comfort in all of this is that at one time or another, we all suck at life.

So here's the thing. If your instincts are telling you that your marriage isn't working, and no matter what you do, whether it be counseling, touch therapy, sex intervention, making dinner every night for almost three nights straight, opening up, closing down, rolling over, rolling under, or talking too much or too little, it won't make a dent. You're like the old versions of a Mac and a PC: you're trying to interface and everything just keeps bouncing back with no connection. It's all just electric air above and between you, transmitting the same message over and over: "we are not meant to communicate." And at this point, it's probably very true.

But do we ever really know when it is time to end things? Some people do and aren't that torn up about it. They even forget to inform their spouse that they've been moving in the "I'm going to leave you " direction until they're sure they have a nice backup plan in place (i.e., a replacement model). I must say this is quite common, especially in men. They tend to like to go from one situation to the next and not have too much down time in between. That would be inconvenient. If there is a new border that has been secured, the troops are just relocated and deployed—quickly. Which in nonmilitary terms means: before his present wife launches a military operation of her own. This usually translates into her retaining legal reinforcement and removal of said children from bunker (house). It can all get very strategic.

For the rest of us, though, it's usually a bit more difficult to accept and move on. However, if you keep your eyes open, if two people have played all their cards and are nearing the end of the game, there are usually some very obvious signs, i.e., no sex. Plus if you find large sums of money missing from your joint account and invested in a company called "Hit Men R Us." that could be another tip-off.

Another sign is when the little things start to add up, and all of a sudden the sight of his sneakers tossed on the stairs or starting the car to find the gas tank on "E" is enough to make you want to kill—him, or yourself. Did you ever see *The*

War of the Roses with Michael Douglas and Kathleen Turner? Detailing the lives of two people on the brink of divorce, there's a scene where the two main characters are having dinner together and Michael Douglas's character is chewing too loudly. Cut to Kathleen Turner's face—a look of utter disdain and absolute hatred. He asks her what is wrong and she replies with something along the lines of, "Every breath you take, every time you chew your food, I want to take a crowbar and bash your smug-ass head in so I will never have to look at your vapid, soulless face again. I would rather chew off my own arm than ever have another meal with you and your pathetic excuse for a personality, and stop breathing so loudly!" Have you ever felt like that, maybe once or twice? Again, that's probably a good sign that things are over if the act of breathing becomes a deal breaker.

Or perhaps the way you realize that it's over is just a feeling of sadness. The sadness that comes from the knowledge that your marriage has passed its expiration date. It seems now that there is no retrieving what has been lost. Then the old adage about sucking it up and moving on can no longer apply. You and it are past the point of no return.

If you want to take one more litmus test, imagine your wedding day and envision yourself walking down the aisle, hopeful, open, and determined. Determined to make this marriage work because you're so in love, and that person waiting at the end of the aisle is the one who will share your one and only life—good, bad, ugly, and wonderful included. Now, here's the kicker. Let's say you know what you know now and you actually have a choice. Which way would you go? Toward the man who at one time you actually liked, with the chance of a different outcome? Or to a waiting cab and the possibility of a life alone, but one that belongs to you and all that implies? If you're already in the cab and even the thought of giving up all those great wedding gifts hasn't stopped you, then ignore door number one, because you've already passed "Go." It's time for the "letting go" portion of our program.

> **"I thought I could fake it but when it came to the sex thing, I couldn't do it anymore. I racked my brain for every possible position and fantasy but nothing worked. George Clooney, Brad Pitt, Donny Osmond. Even Marie Osmond. Nada. Our physical connection was gone."**
>
> **~Mary**

Letting Go of the Dream

Personally, I found that letting go of my family, literally and figuratively, was the hardest part of my divorce experience. It was difficult enough to get used to this new configuration mentally, but the physical dismantling was almost even harder. We were no longer together as a family unit. This loss of solidarity in my day-to-day life was ass kicking. At first, the thought of losing those idyllic images of family dinners, holidays, vacations, back-to-school nights, even grocery shopping, can be agonizing. Everything is different now as we cross over from a traditional arrangement to

a new and scary situation that we've never been in. That's
what I found to be the hardest and quite frankly, the lone-
liest part of divorce. Not having someone to share my life
with at the end of the day. Is there anyone better to have a
good bitch session about the kids with? Will anyone else
be just as proud of an A on your son's third-grade math
test than the man or woman you married? Raising a family
together is intimate and intertwined, and when it is broken,
it is very disorienting.

That doesn't mean to say that a marriage isn't intimate or
intertwined for those couples that don't have children. You
also become known as a unit and your lives become a part of
the other. Unraveling all of that and figuring out who you
are again is the hardest part for anyone. To let go of what
this relationship meant to you and to not care what it looks
like to anyone else is key. Do what Marcia Brady did when
she got all nervous and anxious: picture everybody else in
their underwear and refuse to give a damn. I'm pretty sure
Alice taught her that and it's damn good advice.

Remember the Title of This Book?

As soon as you start accepting this new configuration of family and your life, you'll begin to notice something. It will
suck. Sorry, but it will. But then something else will happen. You'll start defining how you want your family to look
and be.

For example, holidays may actually be fun when you realize that, after everything you have been through, perhaps it's
time to start enjoying Thanksgiving another kind of way
and making your own traditions. Maybe that means having

some single friends over along with all of your married siblings. Or maybe it means going to Las Vegas with the kids, playing the slots, and saying, "Screw the turkey dinner. Let's have all-you-can-eat pancakes instead." It could also mean treating yourself to one day when you refuse to feel any guilt over the fact that you're (God forbid) divorced.

For twenty-four hours, you can just accept it: your marriage didn't work. You tried, you're not unlovable, and you have made the choice to keep giving life a try. Just give yourself a break and see what happens. You might even enjoy it. And remember, as you enjoy the feeling of calling your own shots this next holiday season, your neighbor's husband probably just clogged the toilet. And blamed her. Happy Thanksgiving, baby!

chapter 2

yours, mine, and billable hours

This may seem difficult and slightly perverse, especially now that you are in the throes of your very own little "War of the Roses," but I would like you to think back to a time when you were, dare I say it, happy. When it was you and him against the world and every endeavor the two of you embarked on, whether it was compiling grocery lists, buying your first house, or smugly predicting the downfall of other couples, felt like foreplay. You must take that manic confidence and apply it to your divorce.

This is the most important decision you will ever make— except for your first post-divorce sexual exploit (more on that later)—to ensure peace of mind and financial clarity in the years to come. The time has arrived. You must now assemble your legal team.

The Exciting Legal Process of Separating
and Dividing Your Assets—Party!

Nothing says a party more than fighting over all the stuff you accumulated during the marriage, and perhaps some of the crap you had before. Choose a fun and fruity cocktail, some fabulous appetizers, a rockin' cheese tray, and get ready to want to shoot yourself in the head! Regardless of the economic situation, the division of assets proves to be painful. I've talked to people with tons of money and those with hardly a dime to their name, and I'm always amazed at the junk people haggle over. Many people would fight to the death over a light bulb if they had attached some screwed-up meaning to it. Or better yet, if it would cause the other party significant mental distress and perhaps some resulting public and humiliating breakdown. This would be considered a small but important victory. Yes, when it comes to dividing assets, there is nothing more divisive then division.

Let's paint a picture. A happy couple owns one primary residence, a summerhouse, two cars, some investments, and a wee bit of debt. Throw in two salaries (one more than the other), two mortgages, and a partridge in a pear tree. Time goes by and this once happy couple isn't so happy, and it's time to divide the assets. What would make sense here? In an ideal world, maybe get the properties appraised at market value and one person would get the main house and the other would get the summer home and some investments. Then the one with the greater assets would pay the other one the difference between the two properties so that everything's even-steven. Then they just split up the cars and both assume responsibility for their respective mortgages. They clear up the assumed debt, figure out the investments, and end with a handshake and promise to share Christmas dinner—with his hot new girlfriend no less! Because when push comes to shove (or when counteroffer comes to counteroffer) things don't mean anything, especially if you really hate each other and have ten or fifteen years of built-up anger, resentment, and betrayal between you. Right? Wrong. Hence the light bulb issue.

A real divorce is more like this: both people want to keep the house and every stick of furniture in it, and the accumulated debt is always the other person's fault. Conversation resembles, "Who ever said I liked my car better? Plus, the summerhouse belonged to my great grandfather, so I should just get that by default and the house, too. After all, I put you through dentistry school. Besides, if you think your twenty-four-year-old girlfriend will ever sit her boney ass in my family dining-room chairs then you're sadly mistaken. And FYI, I don't know what happened to your golf clubs or your prized bowling ball but you might want to take a long hard look up your ass."

And so it goes, and so it goes. And so will your sanity unless you take some sort of reality check here. I know people who have changed the locks on the primary residence, hired bodyguards, smuggled out jewelry and valuables (I'm all for that one), and kidnapped the family dog, all in the name of protecting their assets. Some of this may sound crazy, but you have to be smart right now and play your cards right. When it comes to splitting stuff, the general rule of the court is to divide everything fifty-fifty, but things can become complicated. What do you really want? The answer, of course, being, what is yours. Yet the general response can be surprising.

Many women don't stand up and fight for what they want and what they are legally entitled to, and therefore, got less then they should. Unless you are very proactive in your defense, things can quite literally get away from you. Women need to be their own advocates, especially if they have children, because if you chose to lie down and die now, you are not only hurting yourself but your children as well. You need to find out what you're fighting over. Whether you have a lawyer or a mediator (more on that in a bit) you must know what the marital assets are. And if you have heard your husband say "off shore" and "Geneva" on a frequent basis, you might have to do some digging.

"Things" can get very complicated because not only do they have a monetary value, but an emotional one as well. And since as women we are considered to be the "more emotional sex," it would be smart to reverse the roles and run your divorce like a business. Think long term. Is it a good idea to sell the house right now and split the proceeds? If the market is soft, it may be better to hold on to it for a while because doing so would have the best outcome for you and your kids, both now and in the future. Don't acquiesce easily. Look at all your options and make sure your partner knows that you're ready to play ball. If he's giving in too quickly, he could be hiding something that could make a big difference to your life.

There are many factors in deciding how to split the marital assets, including:

- What was brought into the marriage
- Accumulated debt
- The date of the split
- Actual worth versus future business endeavors

These are just a few of the factors that contribute to how the assets are divided. I know couples that held on for an extra week to a year, waiting for the family investments to peak, and then bailed once they did. You have to know the financial pulse of your marriage to make an informed and healthy decision. The mantra of "knowledge is power" translates to any division of assets, even if there is hardly anything there to divide.

It took us almost three years after our divorce to finish settling our finances. It was a fine balance of staying civil with him and getting what was legally mine. Many times I got scared and nearly backed down, but in the end I would remember an expression a friend of mine once told me: "It's only life—and it's a long walk to death anyway, so you might as well enjoy the ride."

What this meant to me was stop being so frightened. Stand up for yourself, because you only get one shot and you might as well be wearing the shoes you deserve along the way. And ladies, if you're surviving this trauma called divorce, you've earned one kick ass pair of shoes (and sorry for using ass again, but as my daughter says when she is eating candy, "I just like it")!

Lawyer, Mediator, or User-Friendly Software?

When you first encounter the whole concept of divorce, billable hours, depositions (talk about therapy!), and income and expense reports may not be the first things to come to mind, let alone hiring a legal team. Heart Break! Bad Hygiene! Weight Loss (one of the few perks) implode inside your head like cartoon pop-ups! This can't be happening to you and your family. You're really not thinking about if your law firm validates parking (mine did—but I didn't use it—trust issues) or if you should be concerned about the fact that they actually have museum quality works of art in the reception area. You're broken, vulnerable, and looking for someone to figure out how to make it all go away. Well, guess what—that someone has left town. And it's not going to go away.

So you're charged with finding a professional who can get you through your divorce so that you can move on. You need someone who actually understands that you don't like chatting with them just for the fun of it. That you are not a legal expert, so they need to speak to you without citing obscure historical divorce cases. That what you think and want actually does matter, and that you're sorry if it seems petty but do they charge you for photocopying? (How did they afford that Van Gogh in the coffee room/espresso bar area anyway?) In a word, you need information. You need information on how to wrestle this demon divorce of yours to the ground and to figure out if this person, this lawyer, is the right gladiator for you.

Now, I know a lot of people skimp on this. They back down, they get scared or intimidated, and avoid taking responsibility for someone who is going to fight for their best interests. Don't be detoured—apply the same demented energy you did to deciding on variable or fixed, one kid or two. This is the time to understand that this is going to get messy and that you need an advocate to get the best possible results for you. Now, don't get me wrong—you're not some pathetic woman looking for blind guidance. You are an evolving single, a supernova who is going to assure that this second act of yours ass-kicks the first one to the ground. And you really, really have to think of it that way. So, like buying a sexy shoe that kicks ass (there is that expression again) and is comfortable at the same time, so should be the fit with your legal team. Do not feel like you have to squeeze into a size six if you truly are a doublewide size nine. Because if you do, you'll avoid them at all costs.

Figuring Out What's Best for You

In this day and age, getting a divorce lawyer can be as easy as doing a quick Google search or looking out the window of your office to the ad on the billboard across the street. In fact, there are software programs that do your divorce for you. Chances are though, your divorce is not that simple and will require something beyond a fast Internet connection.

Before we even get started with your legal criteria, we should nail down what exactly you're looking for. How complicated is your divorce? Are there children? Huge assets? Other women? Other men? Both? Have you lived in the same state or continent or do you see each other at weddings, funerals, and tax seminars? How involved is your relationship and how evolved are your emotions? Chances are if you have already planned some sort of mob hit or alien abduction, you are probably not looking for the same sort of representation as someone who married their next-door neighbor for the company and a partner in bridge tournaments. You really need to prioritize your requirements and figure out what really is the most important component for you.

www.Let'sGetADivorce.com

The software program option really seems to be for the person who married her gay best friend for appearances and fashion advice, even though this too could get ugly. I suppose if there are no assets, no children, no hurt feelings, and lots of spare time, this could be a fallback position. I know there are places where you can get a divorce and a car wash for $100, but you get what you pay for. And again, if it really is just a legal piece of paper you are looking for with no negotiations or no issues, this could be a viable solution. But for most of us, present company most definitely included, this is not the case.

Right out of the gate, I felt (and I was correct) that I needed a fairly big-name firm and lawyer with lots of clout and high-profile cases to make an initial compelling statement. Mediation did cross my mind—and my divorce certainly could have evolved into that—but I felt I had to act quickly and decisively and this is exactly what my law firm specialized in. A lawyer is your personal biographer whose brush strokes manipulate the canvas of who and what you were inside this marriage. And let's face it: you want that picture to be substantially better than the one staring you back in the mirror. At best, your lawyer becomes your legal plastic surgeon. And, at worst, a sad reflection of what this divorce is really going to cost you.

Mediate This

Mediation is a great option for many couples. It cuts right to the negotiation table, with a presumably impartial third party trying to guide the two estranged spouses to some sort of resolution. Mediation can also be a good way to save time and money but only if you are willing to negotiate in a real and meaningful way and don't spontaneously twitch or vomit when in close contact with your ex. It can be an excellent alternative to a lawyer, especially if you are able to put your life interests first, and any feelings of hate and general disgust, second.

Many mediators are former attorneys, and divorce attorneys at that. But if the bottom line is that there are things you are not willing to relinquish or to debate on, then the mediation process, which is essentially about finding middle ground, won't be the answer. Plus, if there are any extreme situations involved—e.g., he's sleeping with your best friend's daughter, draining the common savings account, or doing a reality show on his newfound love six weeks after your divorce—then the whole sitting in the same room thing might not be for you. At this point anyway.

Oh God—I Really Need a Lawyer!

If you are initially determined not to compromise on what you want and feel that the whole process of sitting across the table from your ex and negotiating could be as painful as watching reruns of *The Facts of Life*, then retaining a lawyer over a mediator is the route to go.

If there is one thing I could impart from my own little divorce that really is the most important thing, and quite frankly, the hardest thing to do, is to be as unemotional as possible when selecting a lawyer and when navigating your own divorce. Think of it as "Emotional BOTOX." Just as many women paralyze their facial muscles, so should we stun gun our emotional ones. This is the most volatile time we will ever experience, but there was never a time when we needed to be more focused. Hiring a lawyer or a mediator is probably the first big decision you will make regarding your divorce. How you want it handled is up to you. And don't sell yourself short.

If you can have an out-of-body experience in which you actually are the master of your own universe for just one moment, then think, "I am hiring this person to represent my life and set the blueprint of what is to come." You cannot drop the ball here. And if you can take this one step further, try to utilize a major advantage that you already have. This person that you are fighting, this husband/ex-husband of yours who is making your life hell right now, is probably someone you still know pretty well. His insecurities, his vulnerabilities, what makes him turn away, and what draws him in, is all fair game. Use it all. Draw on all your resources, legal and otherwise, to get you to the party on time—and be prepared. You have to think of yourself as the CEO of one hell of a major corporation, where every decision and piece of information is critical to your success. Be strategic. You earned it.

The Holy Trinity of Divorce:
Alimony! Child Support! Custody!

The Holy Trinity of the legal battles is alimony, child support, and custody. They're the meat and potatoes of any divorce and will bring out the ugliest, scariest side of any person. Remember when you hated your father for backing over your new puppy with the family car and then leaving him there because he was late for golf? How about the time you experienced a little upset when your best friend usurped your boyfriend after you were broken up for a whole twenty-seven minutes? Or does your mind wander back to the time when your business partner sued you for defamation of character because you said he was little "short" and a little "girly"? You seemed a bit conflicted at the time—it must have been the $32,000 legal bill and the fact that "diminutive" and "womanly" is somehow more legally acceptable. That stuff was a mere pittance on the hatred scale. Comparatively, these new battles will make those sessions feel like a love-in.

During a divorce, you'll see your partner in a whole new light as he points out how useless you were in the marriage and how you don't deserve much of anything at all. He may go right for the jugular and call you an "unfit mother." If this happens, don't panic. This is the most common mode of attack. It's the universal battle cry that men use to disarm and rattle women. The first rule of battle is ignore the insults and don't retaliate!

While the Holy Trinity is a separate issue, each actually affects the other. Let's go through them one by one.

Custody

As the mother, chances are you'll never get less than 50 percent custody but there are variables that could be challenging. Perhaps your ex is extremely powerful or spiteful and uses unfair tactics to get the arrangement he desires at the expense of everyone's well being. You have to prepared for every permutation but more often than not, the mother has clout. Now the possibility of seeing your children only half the time may evoke rage and absolute fear in any woman, but take a deep breath. This is pretty much the worst-case scenario. If you have been a reasonable parent with a good track record, you, as the mother, will most likely get more than 50 percent custody. On the other hand, some women might actually prefer splitting custody fifty-fifty or want their ex to have the children more often. At one time or another, haven't you thought to yourself, "God, please take them so I can have a life and work and feel human again." We all have.

Once the amount of custody is determined, you'll still have to figure out a schedule. Many times, Dad gets the kids every other weekend and maybe one night a week for dinner. Holidays are usually split between the two homes. But again, it really depends on your situation. Perhaps your ex wants the kids 50 percent of the time and he'll fight for it. He could also want one week on and one week off. Or, he could try to go for more than half of the time. There are many configurations, all dependent on your specific situation, so you need to be informed of your rights and be prepared for anything—remember—you did find him in bed with your sister!

*And You Thought the Theory of Relativity Was
Confusing . . .*

First and foremost, know the laws in your state. Some are considered more dad friendly than others and some state laws seem to support joint custody more than others. Joint custody is becoming more and more common. One of the drawbacks though is that it often leads to the children being physically shuffled around.

I know a couple that had two residences—one was used as the family home and the other as a guest apartment. When they divorced, the kids stayed in the primary residence and the parents moved back and forth so as not disrupt the children. Situations like this are very civil—if you can do it. Keep in mind that the key to any custody battle is to let go of your anger and do what is best for the children.

For my divorce, I took care of the custody agreement first because it was the most important element for me. I had very specific requirements I wanted fulfilled that I felt would best benefit my son. The most important stipulation was that he stayed in a structured, safe routine. When beginning the process of determining your custody arrangement, consider what's most important to you as a parent. Then, do your best to secure that arrangement for the benefit of your family.

Sometimes divorcing parents are at such an impasse when trying to decide custody that the court must interfere and do an evaluation. This evaluation is a very lengthy and invasive process where a court-ordered evaluator delves into the state of your home to make a decision as to what he or she feels is best for the children. This translates to: you and your family are put under the microscope and a plan is devised for custody, time-sharing, parenting, and so on, and it then becomes binding through the courts. And unlike you and your ex having control, you're both left helpless. The outcome depends on the findings, the judge, and which way the wind is blowing on that particular day. I have heard of outrageous arrangements that could never have been predicted. So if you really feel you need an evaluation process to protect you and your children or the court orders one because you and your soon to be ex cannot come to a resolution, be prepared. Get yourself a good lawyer or mediator (and maybe a therapist) who can help you prepare legally and mentally.

"I never knew I was so
determined and focused until
I had to fight for my children's well-being.
Who knew I was such a superwoman?"

~Amy

Unfortunately, there is nothing fun about the custody process. However, it's the most important part of ending your marriage. It's crucial to establish a good beginning for your kids as you enter this new phase of your unmarried life. Remember, you have children with this person who you quite possibly hate more than you thought humanly possible. In one way or another, part of the marriage still exists through this union and there is nothing you can do about it, legally. So, if possible, be honest with yourself here and try to make this work without your hatred for your ex-husband getting in the way of making good parenting choices for your kids. Providing your ex is a good parent, don't deny him custody—you'll only shortchange your children. Be fair, because in the long run, doing so will benefit everyone.

Child Support

So here is how the old "custody thing" affects your child support. Child support is determined by several factors, including the needs and ages of the children, the earning capacity of the custodial parent, and of course, custody itself.

Your child support will likely be higher if you care for the children a higher percentage of the time (unless your income is substantially higher than your ex's). Because of this, it's not unheard of for parents to try for more custody so they'll be required to pay less. So make sure you understand how time-sharing affects your support payment; it goes down substantially for every percent of visitation the other party gains. Also, child support is tax-free to the party receiving it, whereas alimony is not. The person receiving alimony is responsible for the tax. At the end of the day, child support is something that is based on a formula between custody status and income and will be decided on that basis.

Unlike alimony, which is based on the marital standard of living while you were together, child support has no set limit. It can increase substantially if the party paying makes more money over time, so it is always something that is modifiable. For the most part, kids' extracurricular activities and responsibilities outside of the basic support are usually split between the two parents, but again this is something that can depend on your agreement.

Try to get as much detail as you can with regard to any expenditure outside the guidelines for support. I have a friend whose ex-husband was so cheap that he wouldn't buy his kid's bottled water. Instead, he would just reuse plastic, gnarly bottles and fill them with tap water, creating a virtual breeding ground for bacteria. My friend, being the great mother that she is, would sneak fresh, unopened bottled water and snacks in her daughter's knapsack to keep her hydrated and fed while she was staying at her dad's. Well, he found out, confiscated the beverages, and put them under lock and key. She is at a therapy session right now trying to lobby for contamination-free water. I know for a fact she has better things to do with her time, but this is now the reality of her Monday mornings.

Listen, I'm not saying you have to include a snack pro-
vision in your divorce agreement, but details surrounding
likely costs involving your children should be well delin-
eated. Make of list of all expenditures such as private school,
transportation costs, Halloween costumes, sports equipment,
tutors, and so on. Be specific, especially if there is a big
income differentiation between the two homes. God knows
you don't want your Monday mornings to be about one-ply
toilet paper and budget luncheon meat versus a household
staff and catered sushi snack breaks. The two households
have to be at least in the same novel, if not on the same
page. Make sure you understand the full cost of what you
will be financially responsible for and how that affects what
you require when it comes to alimony. Speaking of alimony,
this next section will give you an overview of the third part
of this divorce trifecta.

Alimony Anyone?

Is it worth fighting for alimony? Absolutely! If you're
entitled to it and it makes a difference in your life, then it
definitely is worth fighting for. Alimony is more complicated
than child support and is based on many additional factors.
The marital standard of living, the day of separation, how
much each person makes, what the assets are, future funds,
investments, debt—there is a whole laundry list of things
that merged when you two merged. When determining alimony, it can get really messy and expensive to find out who
really owns and owes what. And how is this for fun: "forensic
accounting." Have you ever heard those two words together?
It sounds like an episode of *CSI Miami* with all those cool
murders and really hot guys, except it isn't. It is a bunch of
nerdy accountants going through every asset, every penny,

and every angle to figure out where the bucks should fall. And the truth is if there are a lot of eagles dropping, it is definitely worth your while to find out where they are landing.

As with custody, many women don't go after alimony aggressively because they are intimidated or scared or just emotionally drained. But remember the whole knowledge is power mantra? Well, now is the time to implement it. There are a lot of ways to determine if it will be worth fighting for alimony. The first thing to do is determine the minutia of your financial life as a husband and wife. Get out your pens and calculators and start to figure out your options based on the information you find. Some women wave alimony because they get a kick ass settlement plus child support and don't want to be chasing down their ex-husbands for the rest of their child-bearing years. Others go for the bank account over time because they know these men make money and will continue to do so for several years to come. Again, it is worth noting that alimony is not tax-free. You have to pay the tax on it, so factor that in while negotiating.

Because my ex-husband is in the public eye, I tracked his work patterns, and when the prospects were looking up, went after my support and alimony. I must say my detective work paid off. We even had a laugh when, in reference to his earning power, he commented on the fact that "my timing was excellent." "Why thank you," I replied and for once, appreciated the *National Enquirer* and all those tacky soul bearing entertainment shows (which, by the way, I hope to be on soon promoting this book) for my accurate and up-to-date info.

In the end, the fact that I had a clue about what was going on in my ex's life was invaluably helpful in guiding me along the way. Don't back down here—be strategic when considering whether or not to seek alimony. You might have to spend money to make money, but that is the way it is in life and in business, and remember, you're now running your personal life as such. So now that you're officially CEO of your own business, let's talk a little about that lawyer of yours and how much his or her wisdom will cost ya. Financially and emotionally.

The Cost of Divorce (Ouch)

This is the part that can really suck, and even though I've had great lawyers throughout my various battles, I have some serious issues about how much money they can make off an imploding family (you might want to sit down for this rant). The legal system is supposedly set up to help families through divorce. As a matter of fact, it's the exact opposite—the emotional rawness of the situation makes it the perfect cash cow. How perfect: two people who hate each other, paranoid and angry, fighting over everything from the kids to the family dog, each represented by attorneys who can make letter writing and depositions into an Olympic event. My God, by the time all the parties are cc'd on the status of the wedding china, you might as well sell the wedding china to cover the cost of that bill.

Fighting is very expensive, financially and emotionally. And lawyers, God bless them, can kinda be instigators, because as much as they "love" you, they also love to make their monthly billing quotas. And when they start to take your divorce personally (i.e., they're pissed off and "hurt" by the other lawyer's failure to acknowledge their needs), they can get downright bitchy. You need to know what battles are yours and which ones belong to your lawyers and then decide which ones you want to fight.

"While I was waiting for my lawyer to arrive I
asked the receptionist where he was.
"Over there," she said and pointed out the
window as his private helicopter flew by.
He waved, which was nice, because usually
any type of interaction cost me."

~Susan

Just for some more water cooler talk, I'll give you my
take on how I think divorce should be handled. Divorce
should be taken out of the courts and decided with experts
in other fields such as family health professionals, financial
planners, blended family specialists, and so on. Why should
you lose your family and your savings all at the same time?
It is not right! Discuss this with other divorced or divorcing
friends over doughnuts. I'm sure I'm not the only one who
feels this way.

A Shot to the Wallet

Okay, maybe my rant was a way of procrastinating because
I don't want to get into the "cost thing." I remember meeting with my lawyer, who also happened to represent Halle
Berry and Denise Richards, and thinking to myself, "Maybe
he'll take pity on the girl from Canada." He actually was
silent for several minutes after I told him my story, dumped
unceremoniously in a Palm Springs hotel room, holding my
newborn daughter and wearing probably the ugliest bathing suit in the world while my husband of thirteen years

told me he had found his soul mate in Tori Spelling. It was actually the first time I had told the story out loud, and I got the same reaction that I would get again and again over the years. He shook his head, looked at the floor, and mumbled something under his breath. "Men are funny—and women know this better than anyone. You will always be surprised meeting the 'upgrade' (i.e., new woman). They are never, never, what you expect."

After my lawyer settled down, he offered me some tea. An impeccable assistant brought me a lovely herbal mixture in a beautiful gold leaf cup—with no saucer. "With the prices you're charging, can't you afford to shove at least a side plate under the cup?" I joked. It was then he told me he was raising his rates. He also told me he didn't want me to even ask about cost—that was something to discuss at meeting number two. Then he started to scoot me out of there. I had to wonder though, would he even have cups next time? But before I left, I quickly glanced at the long list of attorneys in the practice—and their monetary value. Then I wished for a quick and painless death. How could anyone be worth $650 an hour? And did that include tax, parking validation, or at least my hot beverage? He was right—I was not ready for meeting number two. I never would be.

While extreme (we are talking Los Angeles, and an attorney who has represented celebrities), what you can take away from my story is this: if you go the conventional route of hiring a lawyer, the cost of divorce is high—for a good attorney you'll pay well over $150—and that only goes up, up, up. Mediators are expensive too, and a lot of them are former lawyers, so they know the going rates. Also, you have to fork out a retainer to even get them to work for you—and that's a few thousand dollars, at least. My retainer? In the $10,000 range. Have you fainted or thrown up yet?

Maybe your brother just happens to be a great lawyer, or perhaps your case warrants pro bono work, but most likely you are just like the rest of us and have to pay. Remember, you can always go after legal fees in your settlement—I got them and many women get at least something.

So I think the moral of this tale is how can you get a good and reasonable settlement without going good and bankrupt? It is a good question and believe it or not I have a good answer, but you might not like it.

How to Make It Go Smoother and
Not Hate Yourself in the Morning

When you are going through a divorce, you have to find what works for you and see the bigger picture of your life. It's a given right now that you're angry, hurt, probably sleep deprived, stressed, either losing or gaining weight, and completely disoriented as your life unravels before you. I know. I've been there.

When I was in the throes of divorce, not only was my marriage over, but I could also read about it in the tabloids. Apparently, we were not happy, "a source" divulged, and he was not leaving the children, just me! Oh thank God—I was worried about that one. Plus all the publicity jeopardized my adoption. Translation: another lawyer and retainer, so I was definitely your garden-variety basket case who was barely holding on.

Then something strange happened. I realized this was actually happening to me and if I didn't do something, then who would? So I decided I would fight for me. I wouldn't let my anger overcome me, though sometimes it did. I would think about the bigger picture and what I could do, not the lawyers or the courts, to make this work for me and my family. But how could I possibly do that?

I chose to dialogue with my ex-husband. I thought about our thirteen-year relationship and this person I thought I knew, and used it to my advantage. I created environments where we could talk and work through this, and I was relentless. The fear of spending all of our savings on going to court made me very resourceful. I refused to go through a horrible divorce and then be destitute, and that was some powerful motivation.

You have to figure a way to access your spouse again—whether through guilt, common ground, or common sense—and do whatever it takes to get him to listen. There are no guarantees, but if at all possible, try to bypass some of the letter writing and all the anger and see you can actually work out with your ex. I'm not saying acquiesce to everything. On the contrary, you should know what you're fighting for and who you are tangling with and use that to your advantage.

I enlisted friends and relatives who could communicate with my ex-husband and make a dent in his thinking. I called his sister, who I always got along with, and not only did she help, but she also gave me some information that was crucial to my decision-making process. I also got as much information as I could from my lawyer regarding my options. Then I did as much work on my own as I could. Fortunately, I had a nice lawyer. He would call me after hours (i.e., off the clock) to check in and update me. I never knew which way it would go when I picked up the phone, but he always gave me the goods, no punches pulled, and that really helped me decide what to do next.

At this point, it's very important not to let your anger motivate you to do things that you will regret later. I know this drives lawyers crazy, but sometimes the enemy you know is better then the one you don't, and if you can catch your ex in a human moment—do it. Hell, let him see that you're human too. I am not suggesting you give away your power. Rather, figure out how to make this terrible situation better. If you can possibly cut through all the crap that will cost you money and emotional currency, do it. Whatever you can accomplish within the privacy of your own divorce, it is your business—without judgment. That is reserved for my next book, *How to Hire a Hit Man Without Tipping off Family and Friends*. And don't worry. There's a whole chapter on how to negotiate and deal with felons—effectively. But for now, just keep thinking $600 per hour and you'll be astonished at how proactive you can be!

chapter 3

you're not alone . . . well, you kinda are

You are going to experience so many different emotions via the multitude of stages involved in your divorce that I almost don't know where to start. It's kind of like the gift that keeps on giving and it affects so many areas of your life that you will be surprised where it can rear its ugly head. Nothing is safe from its reach—from running into an old friend who didn't know about the divorce to stumbling upon your wedding dress in the hall closet just before you burn all his winter clothes. Your divorce lurks everywhere at first, constantly reminding you of all the things you are in the process of losing.

However, not all of the emotions you'll go through will be bad. As a matter of fact, some of them can be very good. But at the beginning, it all tends to be bad. "Bad" may be an understatement—it's kind of like a living hell. But hey—at least you're alive (although that may not seem like a good thing right now)!

When it all starts it's like a tsunami blows through your life, whipping your emotions and confidence into an unrecognizable mess of who you thought you were. All of a sudden there is no shoreline and you're hanging onto a tree, as you watch the vestiges of your past life whiz by. "Oh look, there goes my security, followed by all my strength and courage. And now taking up the rear is my lovability and worth as a person." It is a perfect one-stop obliteration courtesy of your new, persistent, and not so much fun friend—divorce.

I wish when I started this journey that I had something to help guide me through a little better so I would not have felt so alone. The funny thing about divorce is, just like dying, there are five distinct stages you have to go through: denial, anger, bargaining, depression, and finally, acceptance. Even though it would seem divorce is just about the demise of a relationship, in reality it completely reconfigures everything. As you're getting this free makeover, courtesy of excruciating life changes, you'll explore some fairly new territory.

It's a reintroduction to yourself. You'll discover things about yourself that you had forgotten or never knew. You'll be surprised at how much you can handle and what brings you to your knees. You'll go through this supported by those who love you, but at the end of the day, when all is said and done it's you that must provide the support. You're on your own and, yes, alone at times, but never abandoned by the one person who should care about you the most—you.

An Emotional Survival Manual for People in Pain
(That's You)

When I think back to the first few weeks of my divorce, it seems similar to a TV movie with Sally Field playing at least eighteen characters (except all the characters would be wearing the same clothes because I forgot to change mine for weeks at a time). I was unrecognizable to even myself. I was calm and thoughtful one moment, hysterical and manic the next. I hosted dinner parties for twenty friends at the drop of a hat and regaled them with hilarious anecdotes about my divorce, even though I had only been separated ten days. And for some reason I was insistent on finding the perfect family Christmas tree—in October. It was like I was perpetually on stage or on crack.

Thrown into the mix was the added bonus of being able to follow my breakup in the tabloids. I remember one particular lunch ruined when a picture was splashed across the front of a tabloid showing my then husband in a passionate embrace with his new love. So passionate in fact that her legs where wrapped around his head. I can/could barely touch my toes! Plus I will never feel the same way about cowboy boots again. Damn.

But I digress: this is the stage where your heart is in your throat and anything can, and will, set you off. You will oscillate between deep depression and total exhilaration. Don't be surprised if you feel completely invincible as you take on this new challenge, buoyed by your friends and family, and then in an instant, walk by Crate & Barrel, remember the time you and your ex had a fight over a sisal rug, and become inconsolable. My personal trigger was my Pottery Barn pillow covers that I bought for our move to Los Angeles. To me they represented Americana, the perfect Norman Rockwell painting, and my dream of being the *Leave It to Beaver* family—you know the one you secretly hated who lived on your block. When I saw those pillow covers just after my divorce, it was pure torture, because they reminded me of my vulnerability and everything I lost. But now they're simply slightly tatty bedding that looks cute in my son's room.

Wanted: A Caregiver (for You!)

From start to finish, divorce is a ride like no other, and you have to learn the basic skills of how to protect and prepare yourself for as much of the carnage as possible. There are things you can definitely do, but the most important thing is to find someone to take care of you! A friend, a relative, an old boyfriend, the family dog—hell, hire a companion if you have to. It's very important to feel like someone is watching out for you, making sure that you're bathing, eating, and at least attempting some sort of human interaction that's not between you and your lawyer or therapist (more on that later).

In Emily Post's books about proper etiquette, she writes very eloquently on the subject. When we are in this much pain and suffering, when grief enters our lives, we need to be acknowledged. In the past, when people were going through a difficult time, the community rallied around and cared for the individual—not rushing the process, but honoring the process of loss and sadness. Good food, warm broth, human attention—very simple things to nurture and restore that person's soul. There was a time to rest, feel, and heal. Many times in today's society, the attitude is, "Okay, it's been ten minutes—can you just get over it already?!" We live in such an immediate society—divorce, anyone?—that if something can't be fixed pronto, we either ignore finding any real meaning in the experience, or buy something. Sound familiar?

Be kind to yourself and take the time you need, especially if you want to manage this little disruption in your life with any future success. Make sure you don't turn off humanity completely. Find the people you feel safe with. Plot your day like an episode of *The Amazing Race*. Avoid situations that are potential landmines, such as:

- Running into friends who might support him over you (and perhaps his new girlfriend—just sayin')
- Places you used to go to as a family
- Favorite restaurants and haunts
- "Couple themed"' dinner parties
- School-sponsored sporting events
- The grocery store
- The hospital where all your children were born and where he got his vasectomy
- The bank with the account he just cleaned out

As you can see, the list can go on and on. Learn how to give yourself a pass for things that seem too daunting, and keep in mind that triggers for your grief can be anything. However, knowing someone cares about your personal hygiene or if you drive off a cliff can make a big difference in your life. It might make you think twice about trying on your wedding dress and going to his office. Human support can do wonders. So can psychological support as well.

Therapy, Please

Maybe you've gone your whole life without a little mental tweaking and the thought of therapy is akin to admit-
ting you are unhinged and crazy. Sorry to be the one to
break the news to you, but chances are right now you
might be a little off. Besides, many people have engaged
in some sort of therapy along their journey through life.
Just look around—the world is crazy. Most of us probably
qualify for test studies on what stress and denial can do to
our minds and our bodies. Many of us don't know how to
stop, how to communicate, or how to connect. So, if your
divorce is the excuse you've always waited for in regards
to therapy, what are you waiting for? You now have an
excuse to get emotional assistance—which you're in bad
need of right about now. Get ready to enjoy hours and
hours of talking about yourself while someone sits there
being paid to listen to you. It's a dream come true—especially now.

I myself have seen many therapists over the years for
minor issues I've had along the way. I have had men and
women, good and bad. Once, I had to stop seeing a therapist
because I ran into him in the elevator carrying four large
bags of double-ply discount toilet paper. When we arrived
at his floor he ran down the hall, locked me out of the office,
and (I can only assume) started hiding his bathroom tissue.
I tried to continue with him, but I could not get the image
of him scurrying down the hall with his bags of budget toilet paper bouncing of the walls. It was okay though. I really
didn't like him anyway.

Through trial and error I did find some great people to help me through my divorce and quite truthfully,

I don't know what I would have done without them. I highly recommend finding a safe harbor to go to where you can talk about anything or anyone. Right now, you need someone who will support you with the professional skills to back it up. There will be emotions spewing out of you like pea soup came out of Linda Blair in *The Exorcist*. These emotions will need to be dealt with before you can move on and, eventually, thrive. Talk to people who have been through (or are going through now) what you're going through. Get names of therapists and go meet with them. Take the time and find someone who is a good fit for you. And, for God's sake, do not be embarrassed or ashamed! This is a necessary step for you to get stronger and better.

In this process you have to figure out what is right and appropriate for you. I saw a therapist, but I know people who see a psychiatrist because they can prescribe medication. I never went this route but I did come close—many times.

> "The more time I spent with my therapist,
>
> the better I felt. Plus he was cute
>
> and agreed with everything I said.
>
> It was everything my marriage wasn't."
>
> ~Flora

I remember being at the playground with the kids just after my husband left me. I was hanging with a few mothers from my son's school having a fairly benign afternoon when one of the moms said, "With all you've been through, are you medicated?" Apparently my story had made the rounds, and after spending some time with me and finding me quite lucid, they assumed I was a little too "with it." When I told them I wasn't, one of the moms pointed out, "My life is pretty good, and I can barely get through the day without them. What the hell are you waiting for?"

These women did seem pretty laid back—a few of them had actually fallen asleep—but who was I to judge? If it works and you need it, use it. It will just be temporary—I don't think you will become Courtney Love or anything. Just be sure to find a doctor that you trust who can access your own personal situation.

You know you have a bad therapist when:

1. He insists that you call him "Frasier."
2. After your session you catch a glance at his notepad and realize he's spent the last hour doodling rainbows and unicorns.
3. He can't afford an actual Rorschach test so he makes you decipher the coffee stains on his ottoman.
4. The subscriptions in his waiting room includes *Juggs* magazine.
5. You spot him at the bookstore buying a copy of *Therapy for Dummies*.

The Doctor Will See You Now

Once you've found the right fit, it will be such a relief for you. I also recommend a therapist for your children as well if you feel they need one. The most important thing is to keep everyone talking. I think you'll find that once you start talking, it'll be hard to stop. You may also find some days that you have nothing to say. I used to get nervous before my sessions and easily distracted, but as I got more focused, I stopped sweating like a hooker in church and let go of my wasp-like ways. I even cried, many times. Of course I would first apologize and try to hold it in, but then the tears would come and all my fears, hatred, and insecurity would pour out. Sometimes I left the session feeling like I had lost weight.

The really amazing thing is, although this was clearly instigated by my divorce, I had a few other issues such as family dysfunction, trust and authority issues, anger displacement, deep-seated and paralyzing feelings of betrayal, and, who knew, dry skin (I wasn't eating or drinking properly) that therapy forced me to deal with. I had to start re-examining everything: my job, my relationships, and I think most importantly, my priorities.

If you are going to get better and come out of this a better person (and really when any of us are suffering to this extent, we need to come out of this experience not only better, but more alive) there has to be an urgency and respect for your time, your journey, and what you bring to the table. After all, you know better than anyone that things can change in a heartbeat. What better motivation is there to grab life by the balls and become the woman you want to be? Can there be a better motivation than the health of your actual living, breathing life? (Well, maybe the "balls" reference, which can be a powerful motivator—but more on that later. . . .)

Support Groups

Right off the bat, I'll tell you that going to a support group is a friggin' fabulous idea—even if you're not a group person. Commiserating with other divorced or divorcing women is a cathartic process. It is the most important thing we do as women. We need to share our stories—the good, the bad, and the ugly, honestly!

When it comes to a support group, you can be selective and inventive for what serves your purposes. Maybe you don't want the typical self-help group that can be emotionally draining and focused on sharing your story. Perhaps you're not ready for that yet. How about a group that supports the migration of the Canadian geese on the off months? Or a group that loves to stamp collect but hates coins? Maybe even that Single Parents for Outdoor Grilling that you used to laugh at. It can be any type of group; it really doesn't matter. As long as there is a bunch of people and a semblance of an interest, you should join. Not only will you have human interaction, but it's also a diversion and something to keep you connected to the outside world so your divorce won't become so big that it swallows you up whole.

When I was going through my hell, I would have loved a group that got together once a month to share the highs and lows of divorce. But what I really needed was to share some of the lows. I wanted to voice what had happened to me and have a sounding board to gauge how bad it really was and whether I should have been more concerned with my mental well-being. I wanted a group in which all of the members could share their battle stories. If we could actually say the words, we could move forward with the "letting go" process that we clearly could not avoid going through.

Make Your Own Support Group

The reason I'm suggesting support groups is that when I first started telling my divorce stories, I thought they were funny. I soon began to notice people weren't laughing—at all. In my hurry to move through all this "stuff," I wasn't dealing with a lot of the things that had happened. That's why I could have used my little "The worst thing that happened to me during my divorce" group to help me through.

A Divorce Nightmare

Once upon a time about twelve weeks into my divorce I was having a lovely time with my two children when I noticed my son Jack obsessively scratching his beautiful head of golden hair. I was at my neighbor Liz's house having our Friday night sushi when she noticed the scratching and looked a little panicked herself. "Hoe,"—that's what she calls me, a short form of Mary Hoe—"does your kid have lice?"

My kid? Lice? At first I thought no way, but it was getting harder to deny the harder Jack scratched. I never had to deal with lice and wasn't sure if I was ready to deal with it now. But before I could express that, Liz had her lice kit out and was doing the comb-through test. I felt sick to my stomach as one brush stroke brought out a bevy of moving and very healthy lice bugs. She quickly gave me a list of things I needed and a split second later I was driving to the nearest drugstore.

Poor Jack. We gave him the whole awful treatment and took him for a buzz cut the next day. He seemed fine and loved his new shorn look. I washed all the bedding, sprayed the furniture, checked my daughter's head and her crib, and hoped that it was gone. During all of this, I became aware that I was scratching my own head! I blew it off, rationalizing that it might be allergies or a nervous reaction to being single. Besides, isn't it true that people with color-treated hair are somehow immune to getting lice?

Plus, I didn't really have time to get lice. I had a big party to go to that Saturday night where a friend of mine was going to introduce me to George Clooney. She was convinced that (in her words, not mine) with my charm and good looks, there could be a soul mate connection between us. Ahh yes. I'm in my forties, divorced, have two kids, am emotionally devastated, and itchy—how hot is that? So I went to the party and I met George. He was lovely and even gave me a hug good night. It was a perfect evening, courtesy of my dear friend Julie.

As I awoke on Sunday morning planning my wedding to George—he practically begged me, I had to say yes—I could no longer ignore my head. I made the dreaded call to Liz, who came marching across the street with her handy lice comb and magnifying glass. Now this is a good friend, ladies—she knew it didn't look good, but she dove in with gusto. With extreme precision she showed me the evidence—I had lice and I had it bad. It was no use protesting any longer.

I made another trip to the drugstore, got the shampoo, and with my daughter asleep in her stroller, sat on the couch with my smelly lice-treated hair and started to cry. I couldn't tell if it was the sting of the shampoo, the awfulness of the last three months, or the fact that the wedding would be off as soon as George realized I gave him lice when we hugged. I felt so dehumanized. It seemed my life had taken on a train wreck quality. So as has happened many times before and since, being on my own in these weird life moments, I decided to turn on the TV for a little mind-numbing relief.

The VH1 music awards were on. I love award shows. I always have. I watch them all and so does my family. We critique the clothes, cry at all the speeches, and basically eat and drink for three solid hours. They were just doing the red carpet, which I also love. But not this red carpet, not this time. That's because on this red carpet walked my husband (who I was still married to, by the way) with his new girl- friend, Tori Spelling. Strolling arm in arm, they stopped to pose and make out for the cameras on a frequent basis. As I had done so many times before, I turned around to look for someone in the room who could bare witness to this awful surreal moment, but there was no one there—just myself and my sleeping daughter. I don't think I ever felt so out of whack with the universe and I just couldn't understand why things just kept getting harder and harder.

While this story is extreme, we all have stories to tell. If we actually told them to each other, no matter how bad, it would help us all. Given the chance to share our per- sonal accounts, we could plainly see we are not alone in this experience—that other people's stories can be just as horrendous, or sad, or funny as our own. In addition to this reassurance, the actual telling of our stories is a cathartic experience. And interaction helps us to move outside of the bubble of divorce. In spite of ourselves, we begin to push through.

So even if you're not ready to join the Divorced Single Parents support group that meets once a week, make your own group—and start with your fellow divorcees. Hire some male exotic dancers, set up a martini bar, and start talking. I have shared many nights with my good friend Liz reliving our favorite "top tens." We go back and forth, and just when

I think I have beat her, reminding her of the tabloid article that said I was sixty-two years old and homeless, she comes through with her custody battle for a double role of duct tape sitting in her garage. And we laugh. How's that for a support group?

When Friends Choose Sides and They Don't Choose You

Having friends choose sides in my divorce was one of the most difficult things about splitting up—especially when they didn't choose me. I had no idea that this was even a possibility and that dealing with it would be so challenging and painful.

My then husband and I had just moved to Los Angeles and we had a whole new group of friends we hung out with on a consistent basis. We were already part of an established couple network. As a matter of fact, when everything went down, one of the other wives sent a mass e-mail to everyone to arrange a highly secretive meeting. She took care of telling everyone and saved me the anguish. I just assumed everyone would rally around and support me, especially the women.

Wouldn't the fact that my husband absconded with another woman after leaving for a three-week movie shoot while I was at home with a newly adopted infant unite women everywhere? Well, not if these women wanted to meet Tori Spelling. I can say with absolute honesty that some of these "friends" actually made money from selling pictures and personal information about me. I learned the hard way what some people are really about. I also learned the polar opposite. That some people in your life will overwhelm and restore your faith in humanity with their unwavering support and love.

It really is a house of cards at the beginning of the breakup and friends can react in all sorts of different ways. Some friends will be completely freaked out that you and your husband, "the perfect couple," are splitting up. They'll think, "Except for the grace of God go I," panic, and bolt. Often times, the female partner decides which side to choose. The choice becomes easier for friends if the men were friends before you got married or if they're in business together. Other friends could simply like your ex-husband more than they like you and it makes more sense for them socially to align themselves with him. Some men could actually be threatened by their wives hanging out with a hot divorcee and highly discourage the friendship (lets face it—we have all earned the hot divorcee title).

By the way, how can we really tell if our friends are real or not? Let's take a look:

1. You often see her car parked in your husband's driveway.
2. She encourages you to try a diet of pork fat and boiled eggs.
3. She tells you exercise is for wimps.
4. She spends a lot of time trying to convince you that short red hair with a perm is the way to go.
5. Her Facebook page has nude photos of you doing a headstand.
6. She can't explain why she almost ran over you the other day—she claims she thought you were an oversized squirrel.
7. Her homepage is your divorce agreement.

8. She prefers meeting at your house—after dark and in disguise.
9. She blocked your daughter from the Girl Scout picnic.

And the number one reason she may not be a real friend:

10. She married your ex-husband!

The flip side can be true as well—the devoted wife could feel uneasy having her newly single, skinny friend (remember the divorce diet thing) hanging out with her husband. I saw this happen with my mother when she and my father temporarily separated for three years. Dumped by all of her golf and bridge club friends, I felt horrible for her. But the three years away from my father took years off her appearance and motivated her to go back to school for her art degree. So take that, golf and bridge ladies!

The division of friends is tricky for a lot of reasons. For me, right off the bat, most of the people in our group beelined for the other side and I was no longer invited to the fun and fabulous dinner parties or couple events. I was excluded and replaced within a couple of weeks. I am sure many of you can relate to this (especially if there is another woman involved).

Faster than George Bush can ruin the American economy, your husband has morphed into another couple, and it seems like someone else has simply hijacked your life, taking over your friends, your social network, and even your family.

Watching people choose sides, especially at a time when you're so vulnerable and unsure about everything, can be agony. At first, I made very distinct choices about this. If someone jumped ship and wasn't honest with me, she was gone. I had good friends back home who could support me over the phone and through e-mail. I was not going to play both sides of the fence—the divide was too great. Instead, I stuck with people who supported me unequivocally and with these friendships, I created a bit of a safe haven for myself. It was too painful to hear or know about the stuff I was missing and what my "stand in" was like.

But, as time passed, it's become a whole different ball game. I have enough confidence in myself; it doesn't bother me at all. If you're going through this now, hang in there. Even though it's hurtful, you'll find out how supportive your friends can be—and the rest of them? They were never good friends to begin with.

Waiting to See Where the Chips Will Fall

After your divorce, should you force former "couple friends" to take sides or wait to see if they do it naturally? That depends on your situation and the friends in question.

During my divorce, one of my good friends back home in Toronto was very emotional about my situation and pledged her support and friendship. She saw how hard it was for me trying to get on my feet and knew of my struggles, emotionally and financially, with my ex-husband. We used to hang out as two couples, and I was really counting on her presence in my new life. That was until I ran into her in the park, where she could barely look at me. I found out she had invited my ex-husband and his new wife to dinner and forgot to mention it to me because to her it meant "less than nothing." Needless to say, it meant a little something to me.

As she said, "When all of this started, we just decided to never take sides." Her lying caused me to end our friendship and I have never looked back since.

This may sound harsh, but anybody who has been through this knows that divorce not only shows what you're made of, but also tells you a lot about your friends and family. Quite frankly, if you don't want the added "perk" of feeling like another significant person in your life has let you down, make the choice to choose for yourself. You don't have to explain; you don't have to be rational. If your gut is saying it feels bad, then stay away. Plus, when all of this is over (and one day it will be), you'll find things will pretty much settle the way they should. Your life will look very different and it is quite possible some of those friendships won't fit anymore. But there will be an upside as well: you'll be able to see what works for you and what doesn't. For me, it was friends who lie, say bye-bye! And friends who stay are the ones who love me anyway. Who said divorce can't be fun?

"This was the hardest part of divorce. It's almost like the *Sophie's Choice* of the neighborhood. I just went with my gut and stuck with the friends who loved and supported me. Now, they've all become a part of my wonderful new family."

~Gayle

Believe It or Not, Things Can Be Worse

True, things can always be worse, but at the beginning of a divorce, when you are in hell, it's hard to imagine what that could possibly be. Alec Baldwin and Nicole Kidman are but a couple of those who admitted that the impact was so devastating they could barely get out of bed the first year. If you're feeling the same way, you're going to need time to feel this is absolutely as bad as it can get. When you actually acknowledge you've been completely pummeled, you're acknowledging the event itself. Your body is saying I'm not able to rebound right now—getting dressed and applying deodorant is a problem for me and I would prefer to get to know my pillow for a while. And quite frankly, I think that is the appropriate response.

In all seriousness, if you're beginning to show consistent symptoms of depression or considering hurting yourself or someone else, you must talk to your doctor. Professionals can get you through this—but you need to seek out their help.

But be warned. Even when you think things couldn't get any lower, don't be surprised if they do. I thought I couldn't cry any more tears or sink any lower, and then I saw my ex-husband on a reality show with his new wife and baby confessing that he has never been happier or more in love. That one definitely sucked.

What about you? Is it your ex with a new woman/man, seeing your kids more/less? What is it that pushes your buttons? We all have our issues and they are all different. The key to making things easier is to not actually, actively make things worse. You'll find that if you fixate on the crap, more crap tends to happen—and at an alarming rate.

Yes, things can always be worse, but when they're not, take the time to be grateful for the areas of your life where you can still experience happiness. I have applied that to my own situation and you should do the same.

Seeing the Upside

For starters, my husband left our thirteen-year marriage after we had just moved across the country and adopted a baby girl. The public nature of our breakup actually threatened the adoption; I could have lost my daughter and almost did. It was my most horrific, worst-case scenario coming to life. But six months after our divorce was on the books and when Lola was sixteen months old, she was finalized as my child in the sunny state of California.

There were six lawyers in the courtroom: one for my daughter, one for the birth mother, two for the birth father and paternal grandmother, one for me (my new lawyer), and another one who had been kicked off the case. My original lawyer was an older gentleman and I had to fire him after he had forgotten some pertinent information regarding a little legal document that allowed me to leave the state. He still calls me about finalizing my adoption.

I had been dreading this day for over a year but it actually turned out to be one of the best days of my life. The birth father terminated rights, we avoided a long and expensive legal battle, and Lola became mine. She got a balloon and her picture taken with the judge, one of the toughest on the bench, who had fallen in love with her. He also seemed to take an interest in me and said I was his second favorite mother in his adoption court ever. "Who's your first?" I asked. He replied, "Angelina Jolie." Could this day get any better?

I was on cloud nine. And I had done this all on my own. There was no doting husband standing by, no family backup with emotional or financial support—just me and Lola conquering the day—and it felt great.

This is the attitude I suggest you strive for. Highlight the good things in your life and don't get obliterated by the battles you're engaged in. Living through a divorce is going to illuminate strength of character and depth you never knew you had. If you really want to learn and grow from all of this, you can. But doing so is a choice. Sometimes you have to take a good hard look around and see the blessings you already have in place, as well as those you created for yourself. It's important to gain perspective.

So your husband left you for another woman—at least it wasn't your sister. And if it was your sister, thank your lucky stars it wasn't your brother (wait, would that be worse?). Always try to find a silver lining. To a certain extent, you're in charge of what happens. You can't control all that comes at you, but you can control how you choose to react to it. That is your ultimate saving grace.

The truth is that none of us want to imagine how bad things can get—who wants to go down that path? But if you take a look around and see the complete horror show of challenges some people have to face, you can see that getting divorced is not the death sentence you once thought it was. Presuming you are healthy, you love your kids, you have one or two good friends, and you can still enjoy a good glass (or bottle) of wine, you have many reasons to get out of bed every morning. If it helps to go to the worst-case scenario so you can mentally prepare, go ahead. But don't stay there too long. And remember that your darkest moment could very well turn into your finest one. You just never know. . . .

chapter 4

love your children more than you hate your ex

Here's the lovely irony about divorce. The person who is partially responsible for this hellish journey you're on is also 50 percent responsible for the things you love more than anything humanly possible—your children. You're connected to this person, regardless of how much he irritates you or how miserable he makes you, for the rest of your natural born life. There is nothing you can do about this configuration short of making some pretty radical decisions (see paragraph on hiring a hit man).

At some point, maybe not at the beginning, you have to make a Herculean effort to determine what you want this new family structure to be like. Is it going to be reminiscent of a *Jerry Springer* show or more along the lines of Bruce and Demi? Or Melissa Etheridge and her ex? They live across the street from one another to accommodate the children and (I presume) to present a good model of how being civil can save your children's sanity as well as your own.

While this all looks good on paper, you may prefer to take your gallbladder out with a shrimp fork rather than have anything to do with this person, let alone be rational and calm enough to co-parent. I'm not sure how your divorce went down and who left whom, but if you were the one who was dumped, especially for another woman, this is one hard thing to manage. At the beginning of my separation/divorce I had the great fortune of opening a magazine and seeing a photo of my ex-husband and his new girlfriend—with my son tagging along. There was an accompanying interview where the "upgrade" (the writer's word for the other woman) said she loved hanging out with "her boys" and that they "were like the three amigos" doing everything together. My family had been officially usurped. And there wasn't a damn thing I could do about it.

Many women have been put in this position where their children are meeting Dad's new "friend" and it just clouds the issues. There is a time for introductions of the new partner, but that time is not at the beginning of the relationship.

And what exactly is wrong with these women pouncing on families when they're being dismantled? Where is the support we have for each other as women? These women need to put themselves in your shoes for a moment, take a breath, and have some respect for what is happening to your family. They should also pay careful attention to how much their new man is trashing his ex-wife and how he deals with her—it could be a nice little hint of things to come for her.

I could really go on here about how, as women, we have to take more responsibility for our actions and maybe think twice before we beat down a sister, but I think I'll save that for later. Suffice to say that if your husband's new girlfriend has Photo-shopped herself into all the family pictures and you have miraculously disappeared, then this whole "loving your children more than you hate your ex" thing is going to be quite a challenge.

Meeting the Other Woman and Other Fun Things to Do While You're Suicidal

Up until now, you probably thought things couldn't get any worse. But if you're one of the lucky few who get to meet "the other woman" while you're still married or in the process of divorcing, you've now become a member of a worldwide club, a franchise if you will, called "Dumped While Married." Congratulations! Now you get to meet, in the living, breathing flesh, the person your spouse is leaving you for.

Perhaps she is older and less attractive (hardly!) or younger with bigger boobs (duh). Perhaps she is his secretary or trainer or maybe neither. She could easily be the girl next door pursuing her dream of bagging the elusive married man with children and a soon to be discarded ex-wife. Who knows? The permutations for romance are endless. But one thing is for certain, you are now part of a forever triangle—the new wife, your ex, and you. At any rate, this is your chance to get to really know her. Maybe you can get together for lunch, a drink, or a walk in the park. Or perhaps you already have had the pleasure of her company because she's been your best friend since college. Whatever the circumstances, you're about to connect with the woman who will now be your ex-husband's girlfriend.

There's really no better way to pass the time than chatting with the woman who helped destroy your family—especially if she opts to rub it in your face or show you romantic pictures of the two of them on her cell phone. This really is the type of situation where, unless you're highly medicated, the chances for conflict are basically a given. It's sort of like asking Jennifer Aniston and Angelina Jolie to share their favorite Brad Pitt moments; it just isn't natural. But for better or worse, if you have children and your man is intent on hooking up with this new gal, you'll have to face "the other woman." When this occurs, the more control you can have over this situation the better—even if it involves prepared notes, electronic support via e-mail, and closed-circuit cameras. You must be ready on all fronts with appropriate backup to fortify and guide you through this experience, as well as a working knowledge of where the fire exits are at all times, because this baby could blow up at any moment.

The truth is, the repercussions of the meeting can't be known until the fat lady actually sings. I know women who have screamed, yelled, wrestled, and commiserated when they first encounter each other, because this is the perfect opportunity for a major exchange of information. Women do like to talk, especially about men that drive them crazy. This whole UN Summit can be a risky gamble—especially for the guy involved—because the ex-wife may not be a shrew, but rather lovely in fact, with impeccable taste and a keen sense of wit and style.

And what if the other woman is smart and accomplished and has been looking for love and family her whole life and she just happened to stumble upon yours? What if the two of you are similar except one is getting divorced and one is getting married? And what if you feel compelled to tell her about all the warning signs you chose to ignore and she feels compelled to join your spin class and meet for regular coffees? You begin to bond and both wonder aloud why women don't stick together more and have each other's backs. And before you know it, you begin to realize that you've dodged a bullet and that this poor woman is in for a ride from hell. So being the person that you are, you let her in on a few more things before setting her up with your accountant's brother—an underwear model turned pediatrician who does volunteer work for Unicef and local nuns. After all, what good is anything if you can't pass on your hard-earned experience to someone who needs it?

Of course, I don't know how you first encountered your ex-husband's "other woman," but I sure know how I encountered mine. It was a rainy day in January in Los Angeles and I was thinking to myself, "How can I possibly top off the divorce cruise I have been enduring?" Was there an area of misery and humiliation that I hadn't fully explored? And since I was already feeling so lousy, wouldn't it be a good thing to feel twice as bad? So when my ex-husband said I had to meet his fiancé, I jumped at the chance. After all, since they were planning to marry a few weeks after our divorce came through, no time like the present, right? To be completely truthful, meeting "the other woman" was something I had no desire to do, and if my ex-husband hadn't insisted on it, I would have passed up the opportunity altogether. It was all happening a little too quickly for me to handle. But alas, the die was cast and the date was set and there seemed to be no getting out of it.

Forgive me, but I need to digress a little here and ask: has this ever happened to you? Your ex-husband's new wife writes a tell-all book about her life and decides to chroni-

cle her affair and subsequent marriage to the man you just
divorced as well as her thoughts and insights on the first
time she had the pleasure of your company. You hear about
it in bits and pieces from friends and family and do everything in your power not to subject yourself to something
that will surely make you crazy. You avoid the media cov-
erage at all costs so as not to relive the whole damn thing
in revisionist techno-color even though a coast-to-coast tour
has it plastered everywhere. Finally one day, when your will-
power is low, you sneak into a bookstore and read the few
pages dedicated to your meeting. Imagine your surprise
when you learn that when she came to your house, she hid
a knife in the folds of her purse in case you made some sort
of attempt at her life or tried to poison the herbal tea you
so graciously offered her. You were described as "pretty and
pleasant" and she said that she dressed in a baggy tracksuit
and sneakers in deference to your older age and appearance
so you'd feel better about the things you were losing: your
looks, your husband, hey, maybe even your life? Talk about
warm and fuzzy. You start to think to yourself, "Why don't
I do this "passing the baton" thing more often? It really is
quite fun!

So to continue, there I was, standing at the door as the
rain fell all around me, awaiting the women who had profoundly changed my life forever. I scanned the house and saw
the life that had been compiled together spread out before
me and took it all in. I think I probably looked a little tired
but I really didn't care. I waved to my neighbor across the
street as Tori's car pulled up and parked out front. I waited
for what seemed many moments as she lingered outside—
perhaps there was a little hesitation at the other end. Finally,
the car door opened and out spilled my afternoon compan-

ion with two blonde pigtails, snuggly fitted jeans, and thigh-high boots clicking up my walkway. I remember taking a deep breath and hoping for an earthquake, just enough to render me unconscious for three or four days—but it didn't happen. Instead, I stood there, practicing my opening line for the most important meeting in my life. But looking back now, I can't even remember it. I also have no recollections of tracksuits and sneakers and knives or poison, but then again, I am getting older.

The Most Important Meeting in My Life

Really, this meeting "the other woman" is the hardest thing ever, and if you've had to do it and suck it up to make things run more smoothly for your family, then good for you for trying so hard. I know how you feel, because that's exactly what I had to do. My freedom was riding on this meeting. If I hadn't been forced into this get-together, I might have had a completely different agenda. But I was in the middle of fighting for "my move away"—a legal agreement that would allow me to move back to Canada with my children unfettered. I took the meeting as requested to secure my deal without a very expensive and drawn-out court case. So I think it would be fair to say for that Saturday afternoon in January, I was on my very best behavior.

If things had been different and I wasn't so beholden to my circumstances, things might have gone quite differently. As we began to talk, I told her I thought the behavior thus far had been the height of insensitivity and rudeness and that I wasn't some cliché inconsequential housewife sitting in the San Fernando Valley. I tried to explain that we were a real family with a new baby and a substantial history, and there were serious consequences to all of this. But whenever I felt I was coming on too strong, I pulled back for fear of jeopardizing my deal and would retreat into "understanding but sad ex-wife" mode who was letting go of her husband of thirteen years.

I felt she had questions she would have liked to ask about the whole scenario and part of me wanted to tell her everything, and I easily could have. But instead I made a point of saying her journey with her new partner would be one for her to figure out and not me. In good conscience, I really couldn't say anything bad about my ex. This was a no-win situation and I had way more important issues at my door than figuring out their relationship. At that point I was just hoping to get my life back.

On the whole, things went rather smoothly. Although I was tempted many times to the contrary, I went out of my way to make it a clean meeting. No broken bones. The toughest moment was when my husband kept calling her to see how the meeting was going. She told him it was "going great" and joked that we were quickly becoming "soul mates." I left the room on that one.

Three hours later, after asking if she could give me a hug, she left. After she was gone, my husband quickly buzzed by to get my impression. "Do you like her?" "Isn't she great?" When I suggested that I thought she seemed quite vulnerable, he recoiled. I quickly added "in a totally good way," and that seemed to do the trick.

Although meeting the "other woman" was tough, it was definitely worth it. A month later, just before our divorce was finalized, I was given permission to move back to Toronto without any legal restrictions. I put my heart and soul into this part of my divorce. I could not bare the thought of being prisoner in a place I didn't want to be, or going through all of our hard-earned savings on more legal battles. So I worked very hard and did what I had to do to let all of us get on with our respective lives, even though it meant at times doing things I wasn't entirely comfortable with.

Now you would have thought that one emotionally draining, incredibly significant meeting would have been enough, but there was another one to follow. And this one was a total surprise.

Meeting the "Other Man"

One sunny day shortly after my first emotionally draining, incredibly significant meeting, I received a letter in the mail from someone I had never met but who was inextricably linked to my present situation. His name was Charlie and at the time, he was Tori Spelling's husband. The letter was one of the most thoughtful, lovely things anybody has ever sent to me. He mentioned how sorry he was for my suffering, and even though it was awful for him as well, he felt that mine must be tenfold because of the young children involved. He went on to offer his support and wondered if in the future there was a chance that we could perhaps get together. I was so surprised and caught off guard by this letter that I sat on it for a few weeks.

At first, I even suspected the letter was a joke. Perhaps someone was trying to pull something off or implicate me in something unseemly. I was so distrustful and paranoid at that point, I just wasn't sure of anything. But after I showed the letter to a friend and she felt that it was genuine,

I decided to make contact. Charlie immediately responded and we made a time to get together at my house.

A few days later, after the kids had been put to bed, I was waiting for Charlie to arrive. I was a little nervous—I again had no idea what I was in store for. Would he have a knife? Poison? Ponytails? Good lord, what should I expect? How about a great, funny, articulate guy who I liked right away, because that's exactly what I got.

Charlie wanted nothing out of the situation except to get his life back. In the press, they portrayed him in a negative light, as some sort of opportunist, yet he was anything but. He was very close to his family, a hard worker, and a very private man. He helped me understand some of the things that had transpired in my situation but would never dish the dirt or betray trusts. We had a weird bond because for many people, it was hard to understand the surreal nature of our respective situations, and at that time in my life, he was the only person who really understood what I was going through. The best part was, we laughed—really hard and often at how ridiculous our lives seemed at times.

I must say that many people in his shoes would be upset about being treated disrespectfully. But Charlie didn't have a bitter bone in his body. He faced many of the same fears I had about feeling powerless in the presence of the Hollywood machine, but he never let those fears get in the way of his determination to move through this phase of his life stronger and more emotionally intact than before. We would have several meetings over the months to come and I would grow to respect him more each visit. I found him to be a very wise and thoughtful moral compass and always helpful when I needed a little perspective or guidance.

Even now, I would love to pass on his number to all the great single women out there. However, I have a feeling he is probably doing very well all on his own. But if I hear anything, I will definitely let you all know.

The Emotional Effects of Divorce on Children

Let me just say right off the bat that divorced families certainly do not have the monopoly on screwed up kids. Take a look around you and you'll see family dysfunction at every corner. I've been over at people's house's where the parents will have a full-on fighting session as if I'm not even there. They'll talk about their finances, their nonexistent sex lives, the bowel movement following last night's dinner, his inability to pick out the right cantaloupe, and her reluctance to have vaginal rejuvenation surgery. The worst part is, they say all this in front of their children! Talk about dysfunction. The things I have heard or been forced to visualize have been horrendous and most of it has happened since my divorce. In a way it's like you become a bit invisible after your marriage ends. Maybe your friends and family don't see your husband beside you and forget you are there, let alone your children.

A traditional family unit does not automatically equal *Leave It to Beaver* bliss. So please, right from the beginning, lose the guilt when it comes to your children. You can still have healthy, functioning kids even though, God forbid, they come from a divorced family.

The emotional effects on children obviously can be numerous and very different from child to child. Some children thrive and move on while some suffer enormous difficulty getting past it. The solution seems to lie in how the parents approach the situation. The number one issue for children who are cognizant enough to understand what's going on in their parents' divorce is that they blame themselves for the split. They think if they had been more well-behaved or done something differently, their parents would still be together. This causes a tremendous amount of guilt and great stress. Throw in feelings of anger, resentment, betrayal, and help-lessness, and children can suddenly become young adults overnight. They learn very early that things can change in an instant and that security can be a very elusive thing. It can completely alter how they see the world.

That's where we as parents come in. Maybe you fought all the time in front of your kids and in some way it's a relief for them not to be around it anymore. Maybe your divorce was a total surprise for the kids if one of the parents abruptly up and left. How it all went down and how much your kids knew before the divorce can both play a big role in their emotions. If there was some prior understanding of things feeling wrong or not quite right then perhaps the kids have some sense of why the family wasn't working and the feelings of being blindsided or betrayed might not be as strong.

Families with very small children up to teenagers recog-nize that if home was a battleground for the parents, at the very least, there's a sense of relief to have the fighting and acrimony stop. It doesn't lessen the pain of what's happen-ing, but it does highlight that the family wasn't working as it was. Depending on their age, children can grasp how the atmosphere affected their lives and cognitively understand that it wasn't healthy. That doesn't mean they don't want their parents back together in some way or that they aren't greatly impacted by the split. It just means they understood their parents didn't get along and that made it suck for them a lot of the time.

When the split is unexpected, as was the case for my family, it feels a bit different. The betrayal can feel deeper. It's harder to explain who Mommy or Daddy's "special new friend" is and what this special new friend has to do with your family as they know it going bye-bye. Telling your kids about your divorce is a tough situation to get through. When my ex-husband and I told our son we were splitting up, he just sat there. He did not have a clue what any of it meant. Afterwards, he went into a closet with BBQ tongs (for some reason, he was obsessed with them and took them everywhere—a culinary security blanket if you will) and stayed there for an hour before he came out. I will never forget that day. It was awful and surreal, as it is for all of us who have to deliver this kind of news to our children.

How we deal with the situation, as well as our choices and priorities, are critical at this stage. Our kids will feel all the things we do and more. But chances are they're still going to love both their parents and look to them for guidance. So in the telling of the news, and the handling thereafter, we have a huge responsibility. Anytime there is great loss, there is also great sadness, anger, resentment, confusion, and guilt—even if you are only five years old. We as parents can't bypass this stage for our children. They will have to grieve and they will then have to heal. They must work through it, just as we do. But make no mistake, we parents can make all the difference here. Your children cannot be fearful and angry at the same time if they are feeling love—they are two opposite states of being. Counteract the insecurity and loss they feel by giving them concrete examples that the world they live in did not end, it just shifted. For example, remind them that they'll still get a new pair of pajamas every Christmas Eve—it just might be in a different house. Or that they'll still have a standing play date every Saturday morning with their friend from preschool. In this new universe, we as parents are not allowed to add insult to injury by overwhelming them. Enough about our crap. We've got to suck it up and put our kids first.

Your Kids Comes First

As much as you may hate your spouse and however your divorce went down, you did have kids with this person. Believe it or not, there was a time you loved this person, and if you have kids, there is a good chance you were sleeping together as well (at one point anyway). You may have thought this person would make a good father/mother. I bet the last thing on your mind was how to split up the assets or screw your ex out of offshore savings. Now you think to yourself, "What the hell did I ever see in this person?" It might be a good question to ask yourself right about now. If you can, make a list. Try to find some of the qualities that made you decide to let him knock you up in the first place. Now more than ever, for the sake of your kids, you are going to need to remember what it was exactly that you ever liked about this person.

Look, I'm not underestimating the emotion involved in divorce, whether by mutual consent or some horrible betrayal. A divorce is the death of your family life as you know it. Asking you to be civil and thoughtful right now is probably akin to asking you to be the maid of honor at his spring wedding—to your nanny. Unfortunately, right now it's like jury duty—you have no choice but to be civil to your ex. It is your civic and moral duty to deliver a conscientious and unbiased verdict. The question being, what really is in the best interest of these children? Do they really need to know every gruesome detail of your divorce or have a new partner forced on them just to teach Mom a lesson? Is it their job to deliver information from one enraged spouse to another, putting them right in the middle of all the action? Can they possibly ever be forced to choose between two parents they still love and long for? You really have to take a breath and ask yourself: at the end of the day is it really fair to your children to be unfair to your ex?

When playing your role of Newly Divorced Parent, there is a litany of opportunities to make bad decisions: using the children as collateral in the financial negotiations, denying a parent access to be vindictive, brainwashing children against a parent—the laundry list goes on and on. If you engage in this pattern of behavior, you'll see the results for years to come when your kids tell you how much they've been damaged by the breakdown of their family. Children are composites of both parents and leading them to hate or alienate one parent is like encouraging them to loathe a part of themselves. Would you ever want that for your family? I'll assume you said no.

"Even though I fantasized constantly about backing over my husband with his favorite sports car, when I saw my kids suffering, I chose to take the high road. I refused to compromise their welfare just because I was angry. It was the best thing I ever did for my kids—and myself."

~Louise

So, I'm sorry to say that means you are going to have to figure out how to make this work with the man/woman you are now kicking to the curb. And if you need a little help—a nice glass of wine, a yoga class, a male escort—take it. There's something to be said about faking it (for a while anyway). So many of us were already faking it in our marriages for years, so we know the feeling can be a little icky. But this is only a temporary state until we figure out this new universe.

The irony of this situation is not lost on me: at a time when even being in the same zip code as your ex can cause a seizure, you're now being asked to co-parent more thoughtfully then ever before. To do this, you have to shelf any disdain you may be experiencing, no matter what it looks like to the outside world, and make decisions that are good and productive for your family.

Making the Hard Choices

So what exactly does putting your children first mean? That depends on your situation. For me, it was deciding to relocate back to Los Angeles two years after my divorce. Back then, if anyone had told me I would be voluntarily moving back a mere twenty-four months after my very public split, I wouldn't have believed it. But here's the funny thing. Back at the very beginning of my involuntary single days, I went to see this very funky physic deep in the heart of Laurel Canyon. I went with my mother on a crisp December evening anxious to see if I had any future at all—let alone a hopeful one. The cottage was heated by a huge open fireplace and the only other light was by candles. She sat me down to do my reading and immediately told me she saw a stack of boxes and that I would be moving twice in the next few years. I corrected her and said I had just moved to Los Angeles and would not be moving again. At that point, I thought I could withstand the horrific public nature of my divorce and would stay put. She said all sorts of other things too—that I would have financial and career success and that my "second act" would be my best ever. She also said I would have a date, although I have to admit, she was a little fuzzy on that one.

A few weeks later, I changed my mind about staying in Los Angeles and counted the days until I could get back to my hometown. That was one move, and the next would follow less than two years later, back to a place where I never got the chance to give my life a proper shot.

The point is my move was motivated by many things, including my love for California and the fact that I did not want where I lived to be dictated by where my ex-husband was or wasn't. But mainly I moved because I wanted my son to have his father in his life. I remember one night when we were living in Toronto and Jack said to me, "You know Mom, Dad is getting further and further away from my life and sometimes I don't even feel I have a dad—it's easier just to pretend I don't." That was a watershed moment. If things continued with us living on different coasts, both father and son would miss out, and the time that was passing would soon make the divide even greater and harder to bridge. I decided to move back, and it is the best thing for my son. But after two years of living life on my own terms, having his father around on a consistent basis is a little more challenging than I thought it would be.

It sure isn't easy, especially at first. But you really need to look at things from your children's point of view and think about what they have lost in all of this. How you put the children first doesn't have to be such a huge thing like a cross-country move or selling your organs. It just means you have to find humanity in the person who may be making every waking moment of your life feel like a root canal. Believe it or not, once you put yourself first and realize that you are much more than just an "ex"—that you are a parent, a friend, someone people love and count on, someone who had at one time loved her life, you'll start to build up the resources to live your life fully. And soon this root canal of yours will begin to feel like a mere scrub and polish.

Raising Healthy, Happy Children— "Broken Home" Be Damned

What often happens, especially in a messy divorce, is that everybody starts to know everything about your life, your ex's life, and yes, even the lives of your children. It's a great opportunity for those who are presumably part of "intact" families to start commenting on the emotional well-being of your kids. They'll be scrutinized, and at times, unfairly. It's all part of your private world becoming public fodder. The first practical thing you can do for your kids is to try to restore a little mystery surrounding your family unit.

I experienced scrutiny and attention to the nth degree, but even if you live in a small town, your divorce could be big news. Your kids' friends' parents may grill you for details. Other women you know may try to pounce on your suddenly single ex. You might be on the receiving end of some curious or obnoxiously sympathetic glances at the supermarket. Suddenly, it's like your family's business is fair game.

For me, it was all that—and then some. I remember one of my best friends being chased down by the *National Enquirer* in my hometown of Toronto. Several tabloids called my family, waving cash for a little heartache. I was offered a reality show to document every moment of my pain and suffering. Every article I saw claimed that I was at least in my mid-sixties. I was painted with the broad strokes of being that cliché first wife who hangs in there and gets put out to pasture when the new and improved version comes along. I had no idea I was so pathetic until I was reminded again and again how one-dimensional my life really was. I became the "older woman" who was "dumped" for the younger and far richer Tori Spelling. It was as if my whole life meant nothing in the face of this little split-up. Have you ever felt like that? When your whole identity becomes your divorce?

We've all been there. Operating from this vantage point, where we feel less than human, we're stripped of any vestige of power we have left. If we want to help our kids cope with things in a real way, we have to do the same for ourselves. Surround yourself with people who see the big picture of what's best for your family, and not people who just hate your ex's guts. Having someone who can point out some of your ex's positive parenting skills can be surprisingly helpful. It can be a relief to momentarily push aside your feelings of disdain and possibly go so far as to remember why you weren't crazy to have hooked up in the first place. Getting yourself to this juncture can be very helpful in the day-to-day process of guiding your kids through this difficult emotional transition. Not that it will be easy or that you'll ever be there 100 percent, but recognizing that co-parenting is in the best interest of your kids is a great start.

Let "the Enemy" In

Assuming that your ex wants to be involved, you should let him. I know your first instinct is to run for the hills and do everything possible to get away from this person, but for your children, keep your feet planted on solid ground. They need both parents. You have to let your children acclimate to their father's new life apart from you. I know that even saying it sucks, let alone doing it. And at first it is excruciating. Sending your kids out the door holding their little suitcases to spend a few days at their dad's house is beyond horrible. It is not supposed to be like this, and everything about it feels terribly unnatural and sad.

But this two-household family is now their reality as well as yours, and the faster you get onboard with this fact, the more tolerable it will get. It is the most practical, basic thing you can do for your children: accepting, and yes even supporting the time they spend with the other parent. It's the day-to-day living and promoting that routine that will get your family back on track quicker than anything else. And to do that it's helpful if you don't block out 50 percent of that equation.

The Changing Landscape of Your Family

Now for you. When that transition happens and you don't quite feel "empowered" or up to dealing with your ex on your own, have someone there for the handoff. Having a friend or family member there when you hand over your kids to your ex for the weekend can reassure you that you're not so alone. I always use that strategy when I have to do a handoff at the airport. I find that being on my own is way too scary, and reminiscent of some bad Lifetime movie—and I know Lifetime movies. So I try to plan ahead and figure out what I might be up against and what could catch me off guard. It was worse at the beginning. But as time goes by, we all get better at this. Our radar improves and we're able to avoid emotional land mines and potentially volatile situations.

For now, it is imperative to acknowledge that even though your geography has changed, your family is strong enough to handle the fact that you no longer live full-time under the same roof. You have to restore dignity and discretion back into your family unit, and to do this you have to show your children how this is done. You cannot trash your ex to the children. You cannot cut him out of their lives to spite him. And you must not take out billboards to tell the outside world what a douche your ex is/was.

Now, don't get me wrong. I highly recommend this type of financial outlay if you don't have children. A confident, bold statement over a bus shelter or to the side of the highway can be a nice way to say, "thanks for all the pain and suffering ass----." But unless you're childless and have great advertising connections, please respect your family and yourself and don't divulge things that could damage or polarize what is left of your family unit.

"I tried to explain to my ex-husband that showing up at the school play with his new girlfriend who was wearing a skimpy dress was inappropriate parenting. He said I was just bitter because I was fat. I said thank you for validating why I divorced your sorry ass!"

~Caroline

One final reminder: if you choose to destroy the other parent, then you're choosing to destroy the family, plain and simple. Leading by example and showing your kids that even though you're no longer together as a couple, you can still respect and work with each other for the family's betterment is a wonderful message. It says the strength lies in the collective and not the individual and that the family is stronger united than divided. Your children need to know that their family is still important enough to protect and fight for, even though Mom and Dad are no longer together. Nothing sends out a clearer message than action. Show your children how redefining a family can be done—with respect, consideration, and a whole lot of therapy.

The Basic Hell of Reorganizing Your Life

All sorts of new challenges will pop up as you reconfigure your family life spread over two homes. (Note to self: get a good calendar). The kids will be bouncing around and so will you until you find your footing and hit your stride. Visitation will be the most challenging aspect to deal with, especially when you have to go days without seeing your kids. Even now, I sometimes miss my son so much, I start to re-experience some of the divorce trauma. If this happens to you, relax. This is normal.

In the last section, I discussed the sadness and loneliness associated with your child's departure to the ex's new pad, the despair we all feel seeing those little feet shuffle to the car, small suitcases in hand, toys clutched to his chest. But hey, did I mention the flip side (and yes, there is a flip side)? There's the elation of having the whole weekend to yourself! No chicken nuggets, night terrors, or clogged toilets to deal with (all mothers of young boys get this one!)! There's the opportunity to sleep in, have friends over, or God forbid if there is a total eclipse of the earth, even snag a date—the possibilities are endless. I remember crying on a friend's shoulder during my divorce proceedings. I was bemoaning the fact that I might only get to see my son 50 percent of the time and how that would just absolutely kill me. As a single mother, she was confused. Was I insinuating that he was gone too much—or not enough? Fifty percent of the time sounded great to her. She said, "I have to pay someone to assume that role—and you have someone who will do it for free! Use it!" After I had a second to mull it over, I realized that she did have a point. We really do need a break. At the end of the day, it makes us more tolerant and better at the nuts and bolts of parenting.

The Trauma of Transitioning

Even with the good and the bad of visitation, let me give you a heads up about transitioning. Going back and forth is the toughest part for everybody, and it takes a toll on the households. Every divorced parent I know has this to contend with. Even though the two of you were married and shared a home, now you are divorcing or divorced. And chances are, historically, you didn't see eye to eye on a few fundamentals (hence the whole issue of divorce), so why would you be simpatico now?

Push your own issues aside long enough to think about it from the perspective of the child who is forced to deal with all of this shuffling. To make matters worse, one home might have a "new mommy" or "new daddy" and maybe even a few kids from a previous relationship. All of sudden, the landscape has changed drastically and children are forced to fit into two very different families. When my son would come back from his dad's, there was always a brutal transition period where he would either be very sad or very flippant. It was confusing and for a while, he just wandered around the house, bummed out. As time progressed and he got better at expressing how he felt, we would set a time after dinner to get cozy together and he would have the comfort and security to cry. Like clockwork, it would happen and he would get it all out—the confusion, the anger, and frustration. Of course, I hated to see it, but I was relieved that he was learning how to let it go.

The time when they go back and forth between homes is the most crucial, and a time when kids need the most support. They have to know you are there to listen to them, even though what they might say is hard to hear. They might talk about their ambivalence, what happened at the other house (which could totally set you off), their anger (possibly at you), and may even ask, "why can't I just live where I want?" They may even say they're not sure where their home really is—heady stuff for a young child.

But for now, back to transitioning. As my son's therapist pointed out, there has to be some symmetry between the two homes, in the routines, the code of behavior, and (listen to this one please Disneyland Dads and Moms) how much is money is given and spent on the child. There can't be such a great divide between the two homes that it impacts the child who in turn feels bad about the difference.

When my son called me on the phone to tell me he was on a Ferris wheel in the neighbor's backyard, I knew that I had a problem. Numerous gift bags later, and after explaining to his father why Jack cannot wear $200 jeans (my parents would kill me—they dressed four kids in consignment clothing), there came to be an understanding that giving too much takes too much away. Not having my son get caught up in the material world of Hollywood was and is one of my biggest challenges. If the standard of living has drastically changed for you or your ex, this could be a problem for you, too. This is something that both parents have to communicate about. It doesn't mean you have to adopt the other person's lifestyle or parenting philosophy; it just means you have to have a conduct of behavior that exists in both households with a routine for homework, chores, good manners—and the same bedtime is a great start.

As far as holidays are concerned, your divorce agreement usually dictates how these are handled. With all things custody, flexibility is always good, because as we all know, life goes at a fast clip and things change. A civil relationship with your ex always helps when you are reshuffling the schedule. And when it comes to the day-to-day schedule, it's good to keep it as consistent as possible. Kids need routine and so do we.

For school events and other activities that involve the whole family, here are a few helpful hints:

- Don't freeze each other out. Suck it up and go to the school play or the band concert, even if the other parent is there.
- Get over yourself and just go with as little drama as possible. Children have a pathological fear of their parents embarrassing them, and it might be a little heightened now in the throes of your divorce. So be well behaved.
- Don't bring the new, special someone in your life to the school bake sale when you know your spouse will be there alone. It is just dumb and plain inconsiderate. We all know you have a hot new partner and you're having the best sex of your life, but it's Tuesday and today it's all about selling muffins for new band uniforms. So please—come on your own, buy a muffin, and make all of this a little easier for your family.

What Do I Tell Them and How Much Should They Know?

This is a tough one. As much as kids may think they want to know the details of the divorce, they really don't, and deciding how much to tell them greatly depends on their age and ability to understand what it all means.

My son was six when it happened and my daughter, who we were in the process of adopting, was seven weeks. Talk about the worst possible ages (although I doubt there's really a good age for this kind of thing). Six years old is tough because kids are on the verge of getting it, but not quite there. And having a seven-week-old sucked big time for me because I was alone with a newborn and a little out of practice. Between shopping around for my legal team, having a full-on nervous breakdown, and seeing my then husband's engagement spread in *People* magazine (again, we were still married ladies), I had little time or incentive for Mommy and Me groups. So all in all, we were in no man's land. Also, because my ex-husband's departure was so unplanned (remember, he was only gone three weeks and we had just adopted a little girl), I had no lead-time at all. What I did, though, was put the brakes on it a little.

I made my ex agree not to tell my son the day before school started (how's that for a reason to hate school), and to wait two weeks until we could see a therapist to help us get through this. I thought this would give us time to work out a plan and a course of action for our family.

What I didn't count on was the introduction of the other woman right off the bat. Our therapist said to wait at least six months before the physical introduction of a new person so my son could get secure in our new family arrangement. With his father not in the home and the arrival of the new baby, Jack had enough going on without any new element to deal with. Unfortunately, my ex wasn't on the same page and introduced our son to Tori just two weeks into their relationship, but didn't fill him in on exactly who she was to him. Because I was so overwhelmed with everything going on, and at this point really fearful of what was in store for me next, I didn't follow my gut and stand up for what I believed in. But now that the introductions had taken place, I felt the truth as to their relationship should be acknowledged. I didn't want to deceive my son nor did I want to be complicit in a lie that profoundly affected our lives. My son was confused and asked me who this new person was. I told him that it was his father's girlfriend and that he needed to talk to his dad about her. Well, he did, and my ex lied and told Jack that he didn't have a girlfriend. Then I had to stand there while my seven-year-old confronted me and called me a liar!

To this day, it still gets me angry, and not standing up to it all is the biggest regret I have in the divorce. In the throes of divorce you can become quite fearful, and every move can have serious repercussions. At times, you're not sure what is the right call. In this case I learned a very important lesson. My vision of the truth and what it meant to myself and my family was important and worth fighting for. But at the moment I couldn't fight. Months later, we went to a great, no-nonsense therapist to address this issue, as well as my ex-husband's upcoming wedding (one month after our divorce was final, I should add). The therapist hit it right on the head when she asked my son, "What feels worse—your daddy having a new girlfriend/wife, or the fact that he lied to you about her?" She got right to the absolute heart of the matter. And the truth is, my son couldn't answer.

And herein rests the dilemma. How much should your children know about the details of the divorce, and what should you tell them? Again, it depends on their age. But while some things will go over their heads, the truth is always the best option. Not the hard-core, messy truth, but a respectful truth that doesn't tangle you up in a nest of lies. The worst thing you can do is to lie to your child on a continual basis. After all, right now, more than ever, you're trying to re-establish trust and security in the family unit. Lying only undermines that goal.

In my situation (and I am sure many of you can relate), introducing the new girlfriend could have been handled considerably better. Postpone this introduction until the new family configuration is established and some level of sanity has been restored (putting the kids first, remember?). But if you believe so much in your newfound replacement relationship, be truthful about it and acknowledge it. For God's sake, don't put anyone in a position where they have to lie for it. If it was your decision to spring this on your family, then having people cover up your dirty work is unfair and damaging. Tell the truth and take the consequences as they fall. If you stand up, at the very least, you set an example of truth and establish that you are fully prepared for the serious repercussions that might stem from your actions. Behaving this way says, "I understand that my behavior has a serious and lasting impact on your life, and I am not hiding from that responsibility." How's that for standing up?

The Human in All of Us

One more thing (and don't forget this): we are all human and we will make mistakes. And I don't think this is the worst thing. I believe our children need to see glimpses of this. They need to see that divorce affects us and makes us hurt just like they do. If there is no remorse, what kind of message does that send out about their family and what they have lost? This doesn't mean you have to share the hard-core details of how you found Daddy playing hide-and-seek with the lady next door. It just means you can certainly tell them you're sad that Daddy has left and you wish things were different, but the one thing that hasn't changed is how much you love them and that you'll get through. You are human, and even in front of your children, you are allowed at times to be so. They will see you break from time to time.

For me, I get the most upset around my son when I have to unclog the toilet. It seems to be the time when all my frustration comes out. It always happens at the end of the day when I might be stressed and tired of doing everything by myself. I know I have even blamed my ex-husband once or twice for the overflow. It's then that I fantasize about having a man around the house to step in and love me enough to grab that plunger from my hand and simply take over. But when that doesn't happen, I get more upset than I probably should, and plunging a clogged toilet seems to become a metaphor for my life. Of course, my son is too young to understand all the ancillary emotion involved in this. Why would he? He's only ten. But he is smart and wise enough to understand that sometimes for Mommy, doing it all on her own is a bit tough. He gets it. I can't say he doesn't appear a little nervous if he sees me frantically looking for the plunger, but for now at least, he keeps me company and applauds my efforts. I think he understands that sometimes even mommies need a little support—even in the oddest of places.

chapter 5

getting your groove back,
one excrutiating step at a time

If you've been going pound for pound with me so far, and at times uttering, "Amen, sister!" I'll assume you've been on your own little divorce cruise. Everything we've discussed so far has been somewhat of a roller coaster: from the day the split is christened, to separate homes, custody battles, alimony disputes, counseling sessions, new partners, old partners, legal teams, nervous breakdowns, and general public horror and humiliations. We've been going nonstop since this whole divorce cruise started. Our adrenalin has been on high alert and running 24-7 with our solar plexus taking the brunt of the body blows. Emotional stability and survival is the dish of the day. We aren't even near the point of trying to figure out how to "thrive" during this period. As a matter of fact, right about now "thriving" can seem like snagging a good parking spot at our court-mandated anger management sessions—our expectations have become so low.

Dare I say it? The most commonly referenced word to describe a woman's demeanor and general behavior during this time (that is printable) is bitch. We are miserable and embittered shrews if we have the nerve to be angry over what has happened to our family. And, as we are told again and again, nobody loves a bitch. It really is a horrible dynamic. I had no idea I was such a people pleaser until my divorce. Trust me—this is something I never would have figured out about myself in any other situation. I found it very hard to follow through even at times when I was very angry. I didn't want to come across like a ball buster, because in truth the last thing I was feeling was empowered. And when I did stand up for myself, it was acknowledged as a negative thing. I was seen as angry and incompetent instead of admirable for doing what was best for my family.

This dynamic leaves women feeling very torn. We want to be strong enough to win this war, but in a strange way, it reinforces how unlovable we feel during the divorce. If we're tough and play it like a man, we're seen as cold and vindictive. And if we show our vulnerability and neediness, then we are weak and pathetic. No wonder there are women out there who choose to back over their husbands with a car. We are sent very mixed messages about how a woman is supposed to behave!

Speaking of behavior, if we manage to come through all this crap with a pulse and a smidgen of hope, then we need to do a serious realignment. Think of this as your chiropractic life adjustment. Clearly, your old life is gone. Or, perhaps I should say that it's altered since that sounds a little softer. We've entered a new phase now and there is no denying it. So really there are two clear choices. One is to fight it every step of the way and long for a life that no longer exists. Bear in mind that if you choose this option, give yourself about six months for your ensuing nervous breakdown, followed by your involuntary confinement. And plan to enjoy a lot of alone time!

Or you can choose the option behind door number two. It waits patiently—and no it is not an appliance or a new car. It is the unknown of your new life stretching out in front of you. It is choice, it is hope, and it is the hard-earned understanding that life can change in a New York minute. You know it, you've earned it, and now it's time to live it. Divorce does suck, but life most certainly does not have to.

You're Responsible for Your Own Happiness (Damn)

As Oprah often says (or something like this), "You cannot control everything that happens to you in life but you can choose how you react to it." This really is true. Look at all the crap that has come your way recently. Never in a million years could I have imagined my story, let alone written about it. The latest rumor to date is that I have been selling secrets to the tabloids and plan to do my own reality show documenting my mental decline as I sit and watch my ex-husband's meteoric rise to superstardom. Throw in a public confrontation, jail time, and a house foreclosure—you know, the usual divorce memorabilia.

Yet we all have our own little shop of horrors, don't we? The challenges never stop coming, and how we choose to confront them dictates how we move forward. And in order to move through, we have to assume the arduous and necessary task of being responsible for our own lives and happiness. Yikes!

Personally I used to hate it when people told me I was the one responsible for my own life post-divorce. How could I be? It wasn't my fault my life fell apart and now I had the added task of actually putting everything back together. I so resented the fact that anyone thought that it was even possible to rebuild, let alone have to put the work and effort into getting healthy—especially after what I had been through. I thought "you suffered" just translates into "you are owed" something. Wrong! It means you suffered, so hopefully you learned something. I was quite upset about this point. I thought I had at least earned a quick remarriage to a hot, young millionaire, that all my "suffering" and "issues" would just cease, and that I would end up living out a stress-free existence, in a temperate climate. I was a bit off on this one. It became apparent very quickly that if I was going to achieve the "thriving" status, then I was going to have to work at it, one excruciating step at a time.

At this point, you're probably quite familiar with what it's like to be miserable—it has become somewhat of a semi-permanent state. But as the dust starts to settle, hopefully you're beginning to edge forward into the daylight and looking to occupy a different sort of territory. So, how do we do that? How do we all of sudden become happy? Well, the sad truth is, we don't. Being happy is a process and it starts with your ownership of your own life. In one of my favorite books, *What Happy People Know*, by Dan Baker, the author presents a guide to self-realization and that elusive concept of happiness. It starts from a very unusual premise: living in the present. Instead of rehashing the past and hoping for some sort of resolution, he advises the reader to look to the present and what is palpable and positive now. While he recognizes the pain and suffering that life can bring and how profoundly it affects us, he believes the only way to move forward is to embrace what is good in your life and not to invest in the fear of what is bad.

Can you do that? You bet your ass you can. Instead of hanging onto your hatred and disappointment, it's time to hitch your wagon to another star. It's time to dig deep and get in touch with what is positive and life affirming about us. For example, instead of concentrating on your tendency to expect the worst, try looking at it from a different perspective: your innate radar for impending situations. Maybe you are a little psychic and have an affinity for the paranormal that would never have surfaced unless you had noticed how accurate you were in predicting certain things in your divorce. This could translate into tarot card readings and séances for some extra cash! And how about that little drinking issue that surfaced around month three of your custody battle? Well, you can take that passion and take a course on how to be a sommelier. The point is this: happiness is not for the faint of heart. You have to want it as much or more than you wanted the time-share in Boca during your divorce. You have to work at it, because in the end—it's more than worth it.

> "All I'd ever been was responsible for everybody else and their needs. Where did I ever come into play? This has been the most liberating experience, to be responsible for myself and my potential."
>
> ~Leslie

Pulling Yourself Up, One Rung at a Time

Now that you have embraced the concept that this phase of your life is in your hands, how terrified are you? At first, I was too. After all the carnage, I wasn't quite sure how to shift gears and try to make the best of my situation. All I knew was I was ready for something different. This whole being miserable thing was definitely not working for me anymore. So I packed up my family and moved back to Toronto because I knew at the time, it was the right thing to do. And then I made some different choices that I might not otherwise have made. I decided to take an apartment downtown where I was surrounded by people and close to the school I went to as a child. My new home was a sprawling prewar apartment with original architecture and a wood-burning fireplace. I closed my eyes and imagined myself a worldly divorcee, living in New York, coming back to conquer the world and the people and loves I left behind.

In many ways, it was a huge culture shock. I had just left a ranch home in California with hummingbirds and avocado and orange trees in the backyard where I could have outdoor dinners all year long. My life had been very West Coast, with my James Perse T-shirts, my knowledge of the freeways, and three-hour yoga classes. For God's sake, I almost bought a pair of Uggs! But I knew in my heart that unless I went back home and got strong for myself and my kids, I was going to have a hard time making all of this work. So I left a place I really loved because it wasn't going to help me get where I needed to go—not then, and not at that moment.

Reintroducing Yourself to Happiness

Right now you need to figure out what changes you have to make in order to reintroduce yourself to the concept of being happy. Actually, I prefer the term well-being to happy because it evokes a feeling of health and balance, and if you've just gone through a divorce, any semblance of balance has probably been missing for quite a while. So how do you get there? How do you start? Let's begin very simply. To actually participate in life, you have to feel human. It's hard to move forward if you're so caught up in your own personal drama that you've forgotten how to connect to life.

What is it that makes you feel human, lovable, and alive? I bet it isn't fighting over whose lawyer is more incompetent or if he can legally change the benefactor of his life insurance policy to his new wife. These battles are dehumanizing, debilitating, and keep you stuck. So, using our battleground vocabulary, withdraw the troops and disengage. By "disengage" I don't mean you should put your head in the sand and give up. Rather, choose (there's that word again) not to go one on one with a person who makes you feel like crap. Silence is the most powerful weapon you have, so use it. No more useless e-mails or discussions about why your marriage failed or who was the more popular parent during the divorce. Just stop. The divorce part is done. True, you'll still have to deal with this person, but the marriage itself is over. Now is the time to take all that energy and focus and put it into something else—like your life.

For me, I had to take a long hard look at who I was and what I had become. I was a woman who gave up a lot of who I was for my marriage. I acquiesced many times because on some level, I wanted to be taken care of and not be responsible for my own life—and how many women do that? To the outside world, it looked very different. It seemed like I was in control and very driven, but something had shifted and I could not access my confidence and my resources as easily as before. In my marriage, when push came to shove I rallied and was resourceful, because we had bills to pay. I morphed into many different careers to make the family work, but it was only to get by—I was never fully committed to what I wanted and needed. And what I needed was my own life.

Sound familiar? Now, a few years later, I have created a very different world for me and my family.

But let's take a look at you. If you're at the stage where you actually want a better life, then chances are you have begun to heal. And if you have stopped engaging in the aftermath of your divorce then perhaps you're feeling a little stronger and ready to do the second most important step. You need to see what you have accomplished in the shadow of this life-altering period in your life. I bet you fought for the best interests of your children, probably had dinner on the table each night, and squired them around to all their birthday parties and sporting events. Maybe you went from being a stay-at-home mom to getting a job to support your family, like I did. You may have even sucked it up and plastered a smile on your face when you were around your husband's new wife who happens to be living in your old house and driving your car. It could have been a midnight visit to your ex's house because your son needed a hug, or using your savings to get fair child support for your kids. And how about that time you sat through the school play, clapping louder than anyone, while your ex is suing you for alimony? Over the last few months or years, you've undoubtedly proved that you are fighter, a warrior, and a survivor a million times over. You must now take the words unlovable and unworthy out of your vocabulary and replace them with evolved and deserving. So from here on out, shut down the war on terror between you and your ex and start to redefine yourself as the strong and determined woman you have become. And if you can do that, let's take a look at a few other ways to start to feel good.

Endorphins and Wine: A User's Guide to a
Long and Healthy Relationship

At this point in the game you're probably experiencing a little battle fatigue. The last time you had a release, natural or otherwise, was when you signed your rights away to the family home. Whether stress has caused you to lose a ton of weight or acquire a pound or two, your body is just plain worn out from the stress and intensity of the divorce experience. You might be looking a wee bit haggard and a tad bit stressed, but that's to be expected. Or, you may look instantly ten years younger and be fifteen pounds lighter right out of the gate. You may see this phenomenon occur in the occasional widow. As a matter of fact, I sat beside one of those hot young widows at a New Year's Eve party shortly after my divorce. All night I kept thinking that this time last year we both had husbands and now we don't— even though her circumstances were much more tragic. She seemed fairly calm and had a really attentive and handsome date. I couldn't help but stare and be fascinated by her. Finally she just looked at me and said, "I bet you wish you were me." And I did. I was jealous of the fact that she could start again without having to answer to anybody. I sometimes wonder if the finality of that situation is preferable to the endless challenges of dealing with your very much alive and irritating ex-husband?

Endorphins are a good way to get back in touch with the physical and mental well-being of our bodies. Truly amazing things, endorphins are triggered by neurotransmitters in the brain that release a chemical when encountered with situations involving heightened emotions or physical pain. People describe an "endorphin rush" as a feeling of well-being and calm that overtakes their bodies when the hormones are released. Endorphins can be stimulated by many things. Of course, one of the most well known ways is through sex. But don't panic—there are other ways, too. Exercise, eating chili peppers, chocolate, orgasms (remember those?), fear, heightened emotions, and even simply thinking positive thoughts can bring on an endorphin rush. We can actually trick our bodies into physically feeling good by focusing on the positive. Just imagine if you took a walk and had a bite of chocolate. It might push you over the edge.

The point here is that our bodies and minds have an amazing ability to heal, and we should start to take advantage of that. As simple as it may sound, there are things you can do that will help you feel better and don't require a whole lot of effort. Start with a massage. Human contact is important and having your body touched by someone (well, other than yourself) is a big first step. Cliché as it may seem, even taking a walk or sharing a laugh with a friend can make you feel better. Acupuncture has been known to trigger a nice endorphin release, and speaking from personal experience, if you can find someone who practices traditional Chinese medicine, jump all over that one.

The philosophy behind traditional Chinese medicine is to treat your mind and body as one, dependent on each other for stability and healthful well-being. It recognizes that our mental health is very much reliant on the respect we pay our physical form. After my divorce, I seriously hurt my back from all the stress I was under (working two jobs certainly didn't help). I turned to acupuncture and Chinese herbs to help me get through and it completely changed how I

approached my health. There was no way I could get on the
life train if my body gave out. And it was starting to happen.

"The biggest rush I'd had in two years was
the Christmas party at my lawyer's office. I
couldn't wait to actually start enjoying the
simple pleasures that life has to offer."
~Brenda

The Most Effective Endorphin Rush: Sex
No pun intended here, but let's not beat around the bush.
Obviously some great, mind blowing, endorphin-releasing
sex would be an awesome way to jump back in the game. For
some of us, it might not be happening at this very moment.
And that's okay. Our neurotransmitters can make us feel
good in other ways. I know a chocolate bar and a good joke
don't quite replace a life-altering orgasm, but it's a start. So
is a nice glass of wine. During my divorce, there was nothing
I looked forward to more then my glass of Sauvignon Blanc,
chilled and waiting for me at the end of the day. I was having quite the affair with my nightly glass of white. I found
it really took the edge off everything that had transpired
during the fairly lousy days. As a matter of fact, my weekly
trip to the wine store became a highlight as I explored different country's wine offerings, looking for the perfect way
to end my day.
    I am not advocating picking up an addiction. But now's
the time to indulge in things that bring you a modicum of

pleasure and that are more or less legal. My nightly date with a glass of wine introduced me to a new hobby. I really do love exploring different wines, especially with a plate of really smelly cheese and a nice piece of chocolate. For me, there really is nothing better (except for one of the endorphin releases we previously discussed that aren't happening for me lately). So find a way to provide yourself with a daily endorphin release—a glass of Shiraz, a massage, or a new yoga class. Familiarize yourself with the wonderful world of release, one endorphin at a time.

Sex-Free Endorphin Rushes:

1. Stepping on the scale after a holiday weekend feeding frenzy and finding that you actually lost two pounds!
2. Saying no when your ex comes crawling back.
3. Realizing that you'll never have to visit your in-laws again!
4. Meeting your ex's new girlfriend and recognizing her from a disturbing episode of *The Jerry Springer Show* entitled, "Girls With Nasty STDs."
5. Getting carded!
6. Enjoying a Friday night in bed alone while your ex has the kids and you know they're extra cranky.
7. Going over your divorce agreement—especially the part that says your ex has to pay whether you get remarried or not!
8. Being able to say yes to anything you want because you don't have some idiot making all the decisions for you.

9. Finally fitting into your skinny jeans (granted, you've been wallowing in an abyss of suicidal depression)!

Saying Goodbye to Unhealthy Behavior and Inching Toward Happiness

It might seem a little obvious now, but that whole "marriage" thing really wasn't working for you and now it's time to make some changes. It doesn't matter if it was a mutual decision to split or if one of you dumped the other. Fact is, the honeymoon is clearly over. So here you are, newly single and highly committed to giving your endorphins one hell of a release, open and willing like a newborn lamb finding its way in the big old world. Isn't that more or less the deal (minus the open and willing thing, because you're probably still a little closed and terrified)? So let's take this premise of looking to conspire with the universe in a good way and see what happens.

Nipping Bad Habits in the Bud

The first order of business is that you may have to start changing some of your modes of behavior. Through your divorce cruise, you may have established some habits that you might want to look at modifying. For me, it was surfing cyberspace, and it became a really bad, bad habit. If I wanted, I could spend hours on the computer with my new crazy chatroom friends, analyzing the pros and cons of my marriage and why it tanked. Still legally married, I could see pictures of my ex proposing with his future wife on Christmas Eve in a forest lit up with fairy lights. I could see the ring and the tribute tattoos on every part of his body, snapshots of the honeymoon in Fiji, premieres and events, and the pregnancy announcement just six months after our divorce. Talk about a cruise! If I continued my Internet habit, I could guarantee a different type of vacation experience for myself involving men in white outfits and plastic cutlery! Does that not just vibrate with the concept of fun? So I gathered my strength and stopped. And instead of logging on to watch my life, I logged off to start living it.

So what do you think has held you back, and perhaps even contributed to some of the problems in your marriage? Did you give up on things that were important to you and maybe even defined who you were outside of this union? Perhaps you got used to your own little bubble and chose not to venture outside of it. At this point, you may have no choice but to do otherwise. Whatever path you have been on, the one less traveled or not, you've got to redirect—literally.

Make changes that take you in the opposite direction of where you've been going. Instead of going to bed at 7:30 and watching *Terms of Endearment* for the fifty-second time, go out and see a comedy on your own or with a friend. Dress up to take your child to school—you never know who you might run into. Definitely don't do what I did and put on one outfit and live in it. I wore my divorce shirt for almost a year. It was black with bleach stains and a rip under the armpit. I paired it with baggy jeans and my motorcycle boots with uneven heels. Sometimes I would top if off with a gray shrug held together by a rusty safety pin. Pretty hot, right? No wonder I didn't meet anybody—I looked homeless!

Simple changes can simply make you feel better. Staying at home and going over the minutia of your divorce to the point of nausea is like a slow death. Force yourself to get out of the house for a few hours at least on a weekly basis. Isolation might have been helpful at one point but now it's anything but. You have to reintroduce yourself to the concept of life. I have seen many women take this post-divorce period to try something completely new. For me, post divorce was the time my career took off. I started doing a morning radio show. Sure, the hours sucked, but I loved the job. I learned a brand-new skill and I could feel my confidence and self-esteem blossoming. I also produced and hosted a new TV show and I learned to travel on my own. And I will tell you why all of a sudden I did these things. Because I was determined to never, never again be dependent on a man or to be as miserable and helpless as I was through my divorce.

Simply put, I had to take care of myself because that was the best way to take care of my family. I found the secret was doing it one day at a time. There was no way I could take on the whole big, looming life picture. Rather, I could just do it on a daily basis, making the choices as they came to imprint my life path with the things that were important for myself and my family. This way everything seemed a little less daunting and overwhelming and didn't undermine the determination I needed to get the job done.

Moving Onward

Being miserable in your own life is a powerful motivator, so use it in a positive way. No more driving by your old house where your ex lives with his gymnast/lingerie model girlfriend. Doing this is a complete waste of time. Talking for hours on the phone about what an idiot he is/was won't help anymore either; it's just counterproductive. The more time you waste on his new life, the longer you will be imprisoned by your own. A lot of the skills that got you through your divorce might not serve you well now—you know, the paranoia, running on two hours' sleep and a Snickers bar, fear, anger, zombie-like behavior, and a general sense that you were fighting for your life. Oh yeah, you might want to ditch being closed to the universe and hating all mankind. Protecting yourself during the divorce is good. Continuing it into your new life, not so good. Now is the time for you to actually start enjoying your life.

Uncharted Territory: Enjoying Your Life

Wouldn't it be nice to know the secret of happiness so we could simply bypass all this work crap? Being miserable takes a lot of effort and on some level it can be very addictive. It allows us to abdicate our personal responsibility for our own lives and wallow in the misfortune that we've suffered. You can spend a lot of time living in misery, and I am sure we all know people who have, maybe even ourselves. Trying to find some grandiose definition of what "happiness" actually means can drive us crazy. How the hell are we supposed to know? All we can comprehend is that right now we want to feel better and defining the whole happiness thing could possibly push us over the edge.

Let me start. I feel a semblance of merriment—okay, that might be a bit strong—maybe a sense of calm is more accurate—when I'm doing something that makes me feel like I have something to contribute. I start to actually feel a sense of balance. I can't say it is state of euphoria, but it feels very human. It's the flip side of how I felt during my divorce when I felt like I was being slowly eroded away like a great drumlin or the Grand Canyon. Being allowed to experience the good things that life has to offer is key to us actually starting to thrive. It tells us there is hope for better things to come (that don't involve depositions and co-joined post-marital therapy). Amen!

Now after the knocking down phase, comes the building-up process. Hopefully, that's where you're at now. You have to take some of the tenacity you showed during your divorce and apply it to your own life. I've talked to many women about how to find the joy and hope in living, and the answer is always the same: live! You have to switch into the verb and actively pursue your life.

My mother, who was separated from my father for three years, tells a story of finding enjoyment in her life during the more challenging times. Once, she was coming home from the grocery store and saw her four kids through the window—probably kicking the crap out of each other—and she just wanted to bolt. She felt trapped, as many women do. She was drowning but she was also smart enough to know she had to find some joy in her own life or things could get worse. She started small—listening to opera on Saturday morning, doing yoga way before it was cool, writing in a journal. Then she moved on to more concrete changes. She went back to school for her art degree, she organized trips with her daughters, she volunteered at a cancer hospital, she got her real estate degree, and so on. She knew her sanity and her family's well-being rested in her ability to make herself happy, and she took that quite seriously. So she took one route, but here's a list that might help you move past the stuck portion of our program.

How to Move On Like a Professional

1. Have sex—with another person.
2. Light a bonfire and make sure it includes his driver's license, birth certificate, and first-grade photo.
3. Sleep with his best friend—twice!
4. Stop scanning the obituaries for his name.
5. Discontinue Googling his new actress girlfriend.
6. Get a job that doesn't give you time off to stalk your ex-husband.
7. Have your morning coffee without highlighting your favorite clauses in your divorce agreement.
8. Stop calling your lawyer to find out if you were his prettiest client.
9. Lay off the meds.

And the best way to start moving on:

10. Begin to love your own life!

For me, I chose to throw a Christmas party with eighty guests in attendance. At that time, I had been seriously avoiding holidays and any memories of my former life. I actually felt physical pain at the sight of reindeer, Christmas turkeys, or those endless commercials depicting happy, perfectly coordinated families. Where the hell did I fit in? I owned nothing red and my family had shrunk considerably.

So what better way to define my new life then to define my new version of Christmas?

I bought an eight-foot Christmas tree, a truckload of decorations, and put the whole thing up myself. The tree fell once, but that was okay. I counted down the days to my party and made endless preparations: food prep, bar purchases, personal hygiene tweaks, and figuring out how much cheese was too much cheese.

On the night of my first party post-divorce, I put on a long, black lace dress, gave my hair a good blow out, and I was ready. But all of a sudden, just before the guests arrived, I became so friggin' nervous I almost needed a panty change. What the hell was I thinking? I wasn't ready for this! But once my friends started arriving and the tree was lit up and the fire was roaring, I felt happy for the first time in a long while. Surrounded by friends and some of my family, I chose to confront being single and throw a party in the face of all my fears. This party was my way of taking steps toward feeling better, and it worked. This sense of well-being went a long way—hell, it even lasted until New Year's.

Remember, no step that you take is too small. You don't have to do the big things to feel better. On the contrary, your life has been filled with big things lately and they're exhausting. So try this: Think back to what made you happy, premarriage. What mattered to you before this merge took place? Did you love to write, draw, dance, or jump from planes? Were you shy and retiring or an expert at verbal gymnastics? Did politics, sports, the earth's well-being, or shopping quicken your pulse? What turned you on? Find something you would like to reincorporate into your life and—here's the trick—let yourself actually enjoy it! All this soul-searching means nada if you won't give yourself the permission to feel and be happy. I'm not talking about just anybody's definition of happiness, but the version that works for you now.

One of the best things I learned about happiness was from a divorced friend of mine. Her divorce was bad, but nothing compared to the litany of losses she had endured over the last few years. I don't mean losing a job or a boyfriend but, tragically, her sister and her beloved niece. She lived through the kind of stuff that makes you wonder how people can ever survive. And she told me something very profound about life and living that I still think about.

For her, happiness was a ritual; a comfort that she could access through some very basic steps. First, she would pray (her faith was very important to her). Next, she would release her sadness through a good cry. Then, when she had been in that place for a while and the tears had stopped she would take a moment, feel it, and then move on. After that, then it was time for life. She would throw on her salsa music, count her blessings, and recognize that things could always be worse.

She took time to be thankful for her children's health, her boyfriend (even though he drove her nuts), and the fact that she still loved to learn. And even though she could still feel so sad, she wasn't scared. She knew how to come out the other side. All she had to do was get to the music part and then it was smooth sailing.

chapter 6

table for one

As you've probably figured out by now, especially since your better half is being better somewhere else, you're more or less on your own. You've crossed that great divide between being part of a couple to being a slightly smaller conglomerate. A party of one.

Bills, invitations, life insurance notices, and parking tickets are now all addressed solely to you. No more "Mr. and Mrs." Just a "Miss" here and a "Ms." there. You're single and even the post office is intent on driving home the message. It's very strange at the beginning. I'm sure you've heard of phantom limbs when people lose an arm or a leg, and months after the accident, they still have the sensation that they can feel their limb. That's what it is like after divorce. You often forget that your life as you know it is gone and there is no going back to how it was. Cheery stuff, huh? Actually, it can be. And just because you're on your own doesn't mean that you are alone. Remember, you have you. A whole lot of you.

Phantom Fear

One of the worst by-products of a divorce is that you're left with the constant fear that the universe might cease to exist at any moment. I've talked to many women about this and we're all in agreement. It should come as no surprise. You've experienced life-altering events that affect the core of who you are. Nothing is more personal or sacred than your own family. Whether your divorce came out of nowhere or it was something you anticipated for a long time, nothing can pre-pare you for the emotional devastation it will bring. It's like sitting around and waiting for a natural disaster that you know is coming your way, but you have no idea when it will strike. Existing this way is beyond living on pins and nee-dles; it redefines your relationship with the whole universe. You suddenly become aware that bad things can happen, not just once, but in succession. And no matter how hard you try to stave off the feeling, it just keeps coming and coming. That's why, even when the divorce is over, we expect it to continue.

I equate this to something I've mentioned before—the phantom limb syndrome, where even after someone loses a limb, they feel as if it's still there. This same phantom fear exists in divorce. Even though the court documents have long been filed, your heart and mind are still stuck in terror mode. You've been fighting for so long and experienced so much trauma, why should it stop now? It's better to prepare for a tornado then a summer's breeze, right? Actually, unless you want to work yourself into a permanent state of hysteria with the potential for numerous psychological disorders or a stroke, you have to learn to calm down—now!

Believe me, I know how hard this one is to conquer. Sometimes when I get an unexpected e-mail from my ex-husband, I think our divorce has become null and void and that I'll have to endure it all over again. Except this time, he'll have me committed, take my children, and draw and quarter me just for good measure. Whenever I start to give in to my phantom fears, I go down a path that only means trouble.

Take last Christmas for instance. I had planned on having friends from Canada visit, so I e-mailed my ex to make sure Jack could be with me for the holiday. It shouldn't have been a problem. As a matter of fact, Jack had spent the past two holidays with his dad to accommodate my ex's travel schedule, even though they were my court-designated vacations. But then it dawned on me that this Christmas was officially my ex-husband's turn. I began to panic even though these things were never much of a problem and we were actually good at working out holidays and time-sharing. Unfortunately, my brain couldn't absorb that fact, and I proceeded to go over our divorce agreement, even though I knew that I didn't have the legal upper hand on this one.

I was inconsolable. My friends were coming! I had bought presents, hung Christmas ornaments, baked a cake, and rearranged the house! My divorce was ruining everything! Just before I called my lawyer to plan my attack, I got an e-mail from my ex saying "no problem" and that it sounds like it would be great for Jack. He suggested rear-ranging a few things to make it work, but all in all, not a big deal. Well, for me clearly it had been! I had put myself right back in a place I had no business being in—the throes of my own divorce.

Sound familiar? It's like Chicken Little, always expect-ing the sky to fall at any moment. But really, who can blame us? I've talked to women who believe their ex-husband has been working in conjunction with local authorities and gov-ernment officials, wire tapping their phones and monitor-ing their e-mails. Throw in the possibility of secret town hall meetings debating her competency as a mother and you have all the makings of a full-on nervous breakdown. It's very difficult to shut off the panic button and believe that this person can no longer profoundly affect our lives. Of course, they still can, but it's now up to us how we choose to deal with it.

If you have the misfortune of having a difficult ex-hus-band who goes out of his way to make your life miserable, there's probably little you can do to change his behavior. But you can decide how much you're willing to let your past affect your future. It's important to get some perspec-tive on what is a real issue and what is not. Fighting for your children's well-being and exercising your right as a mom? Real. Staying up at night wondering if your new mailman is a hired assassin to deliver your mail and teach you a lesson? Probably not so real. How to be aware and proactive without being crazed and paranoid is uncharted territory.

Even though we've probably discussed our divorces to death, it's not a bad idea, when embarking on this cleansing period, to run our fears and concerns by a third party. Not to complain and bitch, but rather to garner some perspective on the challenges that we're facing. You've learned very well that just when you thought things couldn't get any worse, they usually do. And to add insult to injury, they're usually precipitated by someone you gave your heart to and may have had children with. How emotionally confusing is that? So, we can all be forgiven for being a little off or slightly volatile. During a divorce, adding the "safe" room might have been a good idea, but now it's just extra storage in the basement. This new phase of life warrants choices that are good for us and our families. Opening the windows and letting life in? Good. Preparing the house for emotional lockdown? Bad. After all, we've been there for far too long, don't you think?

Redefining the Broken Woman

I love the whole stereotype of the divorced woman. The one who skulks around in the shadows, shunned from mainstream society, going through lovers like *The Bachelor* goes through roses. She's dangerous, angry, a threat to stable marriages everywhere, forever miserable because she couldn't hold onto a man. Most of all, she is alone! Get it? Alone! Our marriages didn't work, so people assume we don't quite work. And this is why it's very important for those of us who have survived the hell of divorce to start redefining what the landscape of the divorced woman can look like. People can have us over for dinner, even a couple's dinner party, and we promise we won't seduce anyone's husband or dance on the table, expressing ourselves through modern movement and our ability to do the splits. Chances are, we'll enjoy the company and maybe even bring a good bottle of wine. The only thing we won't be bringing is our ex-husbands. So thank you for the invite. We'll see you at seven.

This phase we're entering now can be the most challenging, yet ultimately the most rewarding. We are being given a second chance at life. We could focus on all we have lost, but where does that get us in the end? Whether we like it or not, we're on a completely different trajectory, and the exciting part of all of this is the chance that anything can happen.

Taking Some Time for Yourself

Don't you hate it when people say "you just need to take some time for yourself"? What does that even mean? Does it mean you need time for yourself because you're irritating and nobody wants to be around you? Or, do you actually need more alone time with yourself to be alone? Get it? I didn't either.

Post-divorce, I was feeling pretty sick of myself and the thought of more quality time with me wasn't doing it. What I've figured out since, though, is that you need to actually stop, take a beat, and to the best of your ability, learn how to take care of you. Remember her? Most likely, you've been taking care of everyone else's needs. It is just what we do, even when it's to our own detriment. You know the old adage, "Happy Mommy, Happy Family"? Truer words were never spoken. And now is the time to make that motto your mantra.

If you're like me, you're relatively new at being your own caregiver. Sure, I know how to get my hair colored, throw together an outfit, and take a multivitamin, but our well-being is a little bit more complicated than that. We're now in the process of writing our second chapter and if we don't take a moment to think of how we would like that to look, I don't think it's going to be a bestseller. First of all, we're now assuming a whole new identity. We're no longer someone's wife/partner. We are a self-sufficient, freestanding structure with very different needs than we had a year or two ago. Back then, our lives looked fairly mapped out and our part in the cinematic version was quite defined. Mother/ wife, maybe happy maybe not, attending to her family's day-to-day needs, playing a role defined more by her circum-stances than by her, going along with the rush of everyday life without much resistance.

The tradeoff seemed reasonable, though: the sacrifice of the individual for the good of the group. The payoff was security and respect of the agreement that if I fulfill my end of the deal, you fulfill yours. But that whole thing didn't quite pan out, did it? Our sacrifices could not guarantee a fairy-tale ending. And it is worth noting here something that should make us all feel better about our divorces.

Hundreds of years ago, marriage was capitalistic in nature, not motivated at all by love, compatibility, or the individual's well-being. Getting a wife was kind of like get-ting a cow—except presumably the wife could clean, cook, and procreate. The cow commitment was more of the dairy kind but it did have a foothold in commerce. That cow could make its owner a whole lot of money. So centuries later, it's no wonder that we are still trying to figure out if marriage is for us. The 50 percent divorce rate is slamming us with statistics that say it is really, really hard being married. And maybe it is so hard because there is such a cost—us! Can we be married and still be us? Good question.

When I carved out some time for me I began to question how I had let myself morph into such a watered-down version of myself during my marriage. I started to realize that I felt like I needed to be a half so I could make a whole. Is that what I had wanted? You wouldn't think so. All I know is at this very moment there are no kids around, it is beautiful outside, and I am back in California looking at my Hibiscus flowers and the lawn furniture I bought on eBay. I have a moment to myself and I am writing, thinking, and taking it all in. This is unusual. Taking time for myself used to mean making myself so busy I had no time to think. Now I carve out the physical time to just stop.

> "Who knew that honoring yourself with the simple act of stopping and taking some time out could be so profound. I never thought I could be so inspiring!"
>
> ~Elizabeth

What about you? Have you been so busy just trying to survive that the idea of actually stopping is way too daunting? Many people fear the silence and forced introspection that occurs when we just let ourselves take the time to let "it" all sink in. I don't mean "it" in a horrific way. More specifically, letting things resonate with you so you can figure out where you're coming from and map out where you want to go. You need the time to assess what you need to do in order to take care of yourself. Your well-being affects every area of your life—as well as the lives of those around you. After all, you're the glue that holds everything together. It's worth your time and effort now to find a big bowl of chicken soup to nourish and strengthen yourself.

At this juncture, some women take an entirely different approach: men. They jump right back into another relationship, hoping for comfort, security, and to avoid at all cost the feeling of being alone. The most important thing we can do as women is to construct our lives around ourselves, and not another man. I know a woman who jumped right into a relationship a week out of her divorce. He was younger, exciting, selfish, and irresponsible. She went skydiving with him, tagged along to all his band practices, and cruised around on the back of his motorcycle. The motorcycle was ultimately the nail in their coffin. She fell off his bike and he inadvertently ran over her hand. They broke up at the hospital.

I am not saying if you get involved with someone right out of the gate you will lose a hand, but you will lose something way more important: this second chance you've been given to rediscover your own life.

If You Can't Enjoy Your Own Company, How Can Anyone Else?

This comes back to the main thing. If you don't take the time to get to know yourself now, how can you possibly be in a relationship with anyone? You need to figure out what makes you unique, make your own choices and decisions, and be authentic to yourself. Otherwise, get ready for divorce number two, three, and four! Do you really want to go through this again?

It's a very worthwhile exercise to see where you're at and how you're handling life's situations on your own. Is your personality starting to come through in situations that it didn't before? Does it surprise you? Being on your own actually forces you to do things for the right reasons— and not just to impress, avoid pissing someone off, or perhaps, even for the sole purpose of pissing someone else off. You're setting the tone to the soundtrack of your life. And nobody can ever force you to listen to REO Speedwagon ever again.

"After my divorce was finalized, I took myself on vacation and guess what? It was fun! I didn't get sunburned or lost or have diarrhea from the food. As a matter of fact, I'm going away with me next year!"

~Anne

A Divorce Nightmare

A really good way to get to know yourself is to take a vacation on your own. Even if you can't manage a week away from work, the kids, and the rest of your life, see if you can sneak in one night at a B&B when your ex has the kids. I did just before I made my decision to move back to Los Angeles. I had just finished filming sixty-five episodes of my TV show in three weeks and worked my last day as a morning radio host. I had been getting up at 4:30 in the morning for two years and I was beyond exhausted and decided to take a much-needed vacation.

I called everyone I knew to see if they wanted a little R&R in the Caribbean. I definitely didn't want to go alone— wouldn't that make me kind of a loser? Apparently not. Sophisticated women travel all the time on their own and have wonderful, madcap holidays adored and revered by all. Or at least that's what all my friends told me when they said they couldn't get away for a week. With that idea fresh in my mind, I booked a week's vacation at a beautiful, luxurious resort in Turks and Caicos. I completely blew my budget, but told myself that I was worth it. I packed books, wraps for the evening, and my iPod, brimming with life affirming music. I would dress in caftans and big sunglasses and meet eligible, wealthy men at dinner. They would see me, sun-kissed and glowing, and become helpless in the face of my sophisticated, womanly charms. I was thinking I pretty much had this one locked up. And I did. Well, except for a few things. . . .

It began with me twisting my back two days before my vacation began. Sure, it was a little sore, but surely the sun and salt water would remedy that. So what if the plane was delayed from taking off for five hours because of hurricane-like weather? Eventually, I got there and the resort was spectacu-lar! A paradise! Such a paradise, in fact, that most people there were either on their honeymoon or participating in a clandestine affair with their secretary or dental hygienist. It seems these people were in the mind frame of, "Hey if you can't make out wherever you want at any time you want, what's the point of a honeymoon or banging your wife's sister? It made lunch at the swim up bar a little challenging—didn't they have a room for that sort of thing? But I rose above it and booked an appointment at the spa for a massage to ease my back pain, and let's face it, to have a little feel-up myself. That's when I noticed I was having a slight problem hearing out of my left ear. Probably just blocked from the flight. Not to worry. After a scrumptious meal, I'd get some Q-tips and everything would be fine. After all, I was on vacation.

When I woke up the next morning, I couldn't move. I figured maybe the massage had aggravated my back. But I remained optimistic. My body probably just needed some time to heal. Several hours later, I had made my way to the pool (usually a two-minute walk) and sat at a table to order lunch. I couldn't help but feel a slight irritation in my right eye. By "slight irritation," I mean it felt like I had a small rock attached to my retina. The pain was so bad I had to remove my contacts and ask the waiter for a cold compress. I felt a bit better after the compress and decided to try to order lunch. At this point, however, my hearing wasn't very good so it must have been a little awkward for the poor waiter who had been trying to take my order for the last fifteen minutes. Not only could I not hear him, but I couldn't see him either. At this point, I decided to go back to my room in the hopes of restoring a little dignity to my holiday. Unfortunately, that did not happen. It seems my scrumptious meal from the night before must have been a little off—don't even ask how off.

Five hundred dollars and a trip to the private clinic later, a few of the problems got resolved. It seems I had clogged ears due to a wax buildup. First they doused my ears with peroxide then proceeded to suck the wax out with an earwax sucker. They tried to readjust my back, but thought the problem might be a little more serious than that and recommended an MRI upon my return home. That stomach thing? They guessed it was a gastronomic infection and ordered me to stay away from seafood, cheese, and alcohol (were they kidding me!?). If I stuck to bananas and rice, they told me I should be better by the time I got home. Fabulous! Throw in the weird couple that tried to get me to have a threesome, and you have the most perfect vacation ever.

But you know what? In a way, it actually was a perfect vacation because I was forced to deal with things I had been putting off for ages. I couldn't see, hear, move, or eat, so if there was a time for introspection and self-reflection, it was then. It was on this holiday that I decided to move back to California, to the place where my most horrendous life experience had happened, and confront it head on. That was July—by September, my son was enrolled in school, my daughter had child care, and I had found a quaint ranch house overgrown with roses and grapefruit trees.

My vacation taught me that I'm easygoing and that I know how to make the best of a bad situation. But more than that, it let me know that I was no longer too scared to make good decisions for me and my family. I was coming out the other side of my divorce cruise. I don't know if I would have realized any of that unless I had been forced to deal with a less-than-ideal situation by myself. It showed me what I was made of. Being in my own company was not bad at all and somewhere down the road, someone else might just enjoy it as well.

Should You Still Sleep on Your Side of the Bed?

I always liked my side of the bed. Whenever my then husband and I moved, I had the good sense to fight for it. However, after my divorce I found myself still sleeping on my side of the bed and wondering why I was limiting myself to half of the bed when I now had the freedom to sprawl. Once, I tried to throw caution to the wind and occupy his side, but at the last minute I shuffled back and curled up at my designated spot. It just felt too weird. Why couldn't I take advantage of my newfound freedom to choose? If I was hesitant to even claim bed space, how was I going to occupy this new world I was being given? We all need to ask ourselves, how comfortable are we in this new role we are playing? And can one woman play all the parts?

So, what should you hold onto and what should you let go? Whether you like it or not, change has been the operative word over the last little while and at times, it probably feels like aliens have swooped down and completely taken over your life. That's what it felt like to me anyway. After all, there were things in place in my life that I didn't want to change, and I used to wonder if I could hold onto these things and still experience the metamorphosis that would take me to the next level in my life. Like the saying goes, "don't throw the baby out with the bath water." Hold on to what works and get rid of what doesn't. Well, I guess the husband thing wasn't really working (we have the divorce papers and our lawyer's bill to prove it) but there are other things in our lives that can help us to get back on our feet. Sounds like it's time for the newly enlightened women that we have become/are becoming to take some serious inventory.

Other Things to Get Rid of Besides Your Husband:
- The framed photos of his mother that she'd send him every year.
- The trashy porn that he saved on the computer.
- The wood paneling in the den.
- His collection of bass fishing magazines that he was convinced would be worth something one day.
- The nasal strips that helped with his snoring that he'd peel off in the morning and toss inadvertently all over the house.
- The Bow Flex that he just had to have that was only used to house his dirty underwear.
- The industrial scented air freshener that he'd spray four to five times a day in the bathroom.

Nippin' and Tuckin'
Change is a wonderful thing if motivated by the right reasons. We're definitely in a time of flux now and experiencing challenges that reflect our new livin' single mode on a daily basis. I personally made drastic changes: moving

across the country, sifting through friendships that didn't work, trying a new career challenge, changing grocery stores, and so on—anything to obliterate any vestiges of my old life. For many of us, it's as if we want to get rid of any hint of who we were when we were married. Even looking in the mirror is a reminder of our old existence, and that's why it's so tempting to change our confusing exterior. If you find yourself looking for a little change—some highlights, a couple of new outfits, go for it. But if you are looking for a complete body overall (e.g., plastic surgery), be careful.

Hey, I have nothing against a little nip and tuck. When I was promoting my television show, I even did a segment where they zapped away my face's history with BOTOX and Thermage treatments. I mostly agreed to this because I got them for free. My wrinkles were erased and all my worry and anxiety lines from the divorce cruise were gone. I looked rested—and a little bit crazy. Quite frankly, I resembled a waxy, paralyzed version of my old self. I'm not saying I didn't like it (even though it was hard to look relaxed when my eyebrow was near my hairline). It was just that looking only semi-familiar to myself was too far away from my comfort zone. For now, a good rule of thumb is that until you have really figured out this new role of yours, major changes should come from the inside out.

Keeping the Good Friends Close

As I wrote about in Chapter 3, another area to be careful is with friendships. This whole divorce experience has been so emotional that you might be tempted to completely start from scratch and cut all ties that remind you of your old life.

I got rid of some friends right off the bat. Those were the "friends" who sold information to the tabloids. An informer in your house is not really a good thing. On the other end of the spectrum, I also found there were friends worth holding on to. Those were the ones who may have been conflicted about choosing sides but really tried to do the right thing. Usually these were my "couple friends" who could still be in my life without painfully reminding me of how we all used to hang out as couples. I have some married friends who are so wonderful and entertaining. When we get together, it's just three great friends having a wonderful time, and I never feel like the third wheel. Sometimes I don't even mind the odd marital spat because it makes me momentarily thankful that I am not still married. I've forged a new dynamic in these relationships. We spend time as a trio because we all really like each other. And they never make me feel bad that I arrive and leave solo.

Although you may be tempted to toss out friends who have let you down, you may want to think twice. One of my best friends who I was really counting on for support went a bit AWOL when I moved back to Canada. We went four months without talking, the longest we'd ever gone, and I was so angry I couldn't call her or write her. She finally made the first move and asked if she could come to my house for a Christmas drink. After that first cocktail, it all came out. It seemed her husband never really liked me and felt that I, in my present single state, would lead his wife down the evil path of a wanton divorced hussy. He was uncomfortable with my new position in life and thought it was contagious. My friend was in a terrible bind and didn't even pretend that what her partner was doing was justified—she knew it wasn't. What she did say was that she loved and treasured our friendship but that her life was complicated. At that time, what she could give me was limited, but she wanted to be in my life. How could I walk away from that? She was honest and I respected that. As time progressed we became closer and closer, especially since her husband saw that I didn't sell her into forced prostitution. Since I moved back to California, she is one of the people I miss the most. The friends who have stuck by you over the years are pretty irreplaceable.

Studies show that married men live about ten years longer than unmarried men (my personal theory is that they suck out our life blood) and unmarried women don't show a significant difference from married females. As a matter of fact, studies show that if women have a solid arsenal of female friends, not only do they live longer, but they also experience less depression. It seems our bond with other females (highlighted by communication and commiseration) can actually enrich and profoundly affect our mental and physical health in a positive way. So before you try to close yourself off from your friends who you fear may not be able to relate to your divorce, think about how your relationship can benefit both of you.

Holding On to You

There's another thing in the bath water that you might miss if you just toss it away—yourself, to be specific. I know you may be tempted to unload all the baggage that you have been carrying around since your divorce. And who could blame you? Men make changes all the time. Often it's the middle-age three-part package: a sports car, a wardrobe better suited for a toddler, and a younger woman. So why can't we have a little fun, too?

We can! You just need to remember, especially now, that even though your marriage failed, it does not mean you are a failure. Sure, we could all use a little tweaking, but don't throw away the things you liked about yourself just because your ex didn't. So go ahead—deviate a little. Rent a sports car and hide the minivan in the garage, invest in some slightly provocative (i.e., slutty) clothing and be open to the charms of younger men (and there are many)! If you feel like it and can afford it, have a bit of BOTOX. Enjoy yourself. You're no longer on a day pass. This is your life and you are in charge. Imagine that: no arguments tonight over your inability to fold his underwear correctly. Open-minded, experienced, and a little crazy is one hell of a good combination!

Some Great Things about Being by Yourself

Going through a divorce can be very isolating and lonely but you can have the same feelings being trapped in an unhealthy relationship. If the marriage is not working, there are very few holistic benefits. Maybe this is true of you. Perhaps you were saddled with your partner's demands but frozen out of the communication and commiseration part. For many people, marriage was like babysitting and never getting paid—ever. And that sucks.

So at this juncture I want you to recognize that there are many wonderful things about being by yourself. I'll start by sharing how I finally learned this lesson. When I was married, my ex-husband used to leave half-finished cups of coffee all around the house. They would sit there for hours and the cream would congeal all along the sides of the cup and often I would forget where one was and accidentally knock it over. A few times I chose to dump them but the wrath was so harsh I would just leave well enough alone.

One time, when my friend was visiting us in Los Angeles, she not only unknowingly moved the coffee cup, but also chose to wash it and put it away. When my ex discovered what she had done, he confronted her. She tried to explain that she didn't know he was still enjoying his morning coffee and she was very sorry. I could see her bottom lip quiver as she tried to regain her composure in the face of a caffeine-deficiency tirade. I quickly ran into the kitchen, poured a new cup of coffee, and did what every good WASP does—talked about the weather and shuffled her out. Now I don't have to put up with that. In fact, if someone comes over and doesn't drink all of their coffee before it gets cold, it's gone. Don't even get me started on the mugs—my guests lose all mug privileges if they start taking up real estate! After all, they're my coffee cups now and I get to call the caffeine shots.

The coffee example is just a small thing, but it's actually quite significant in how I want my life to be. I aspire to a relaxed, even-keeled household with minimal drama and not a remake of *Raging Bull* taking over. I love going to parties on my own, hailing a cab just for me, and my small purse holding just a little cash and a tube of red lipstick. I feel younger and more free. I enjoy not feeling like I always have to answer to someone else. I organize the fridge the way I want, rip open a cereal box from the bottom up, talk for hours on the phone to my dearest friends about the stupidest things, and never have to listen to anyone tell me what I'm doing is wrong. I also no longer have to hang out with people I never clicked with just because I was part of a twosome.

And let's not forget about not having to see the in-laws for significant periods of time during the holidays. That in itself is almost worth the price of divorce. I have a friend whose husband's family never uttered a word to her in the fifteen years they were together. No wonder she felt confident in her decision to never see them again. Who needs that animosity?

Where does it all fall for you? If you're honest with yourself as the years spilled by, you were probably longing for a part of your life that was earmarked just for you. Well, here it is! A brand-spanking new life, ready to be explored. Who cares if you got the opportunity courtesy of your miserable divorce? Don't look a gift horse in the mouth—take it! Spend some time imagining some of the great things about being on your own, especially after years of being lost in the world of couples and groups.

Think about it—you can:

- Turn his home office with the wood paneling and forest green walls into a quiet room—just paint over everything.
- Clear out the garage of all the sports equipment he never used and actually use it to park your new sports car.
- Go to all your favorite exotic restaurants on your own or with a friend and savor the time after dinner when you don't have to hear how the food gave him gas.
- Get rid of all the meat products in your freezer (unless you want them there!).

- Put crisp white sheets on the bed and enjoy an evening in bed, reading stacks of self-help books with no one there to give you a hard time.
- Embrace your lack of housekeeping skills and use whatever extra cash you have to get someone else to do the laundry.
- Clear out the closets of anything of his that remains, and if possible, allow yourself the pleasure of ripping up a business suit and at least one polyester sports ensemble.
- Arrange your environment in a way that makes you happy and start enjoying a world without tension and man smells. The former, we want to say goodbye to forever. The latter—we're just taking a little break.

As I mentioned before, one of the most important things to do after divorce is to reconnect with your former self—you know, the person you were before you were married. Now is the time to start reconnecting with things that used to give you happiness. With age and wisdom comes a different skill set that (hopefully) allows us to grow and learn from life's darker days. Our experience is an asset, but it can become a liability if we let it block out the need to connect with the fun and hopeful side of what life has to offer. So where do you start?

For starters, think about what brings you joy. I have a friend I've known since the eighth grade who always wanted to be a comedy writer. She's one of the funniest people I have ever met and is completely mental in the best of all possible ways—wildly entertaining, full of life, and generous to a fault. She was married to someone who sucked the life out of her and become an almost lifeless, watered-down version of her former self. The sparkle was gone and there was nothing I could do about it. But there was a lot she could do—and eventually she did.

After months of soul-searching, she left her husband, moved halfway around the world, and got a job writing sitcoms—in Singapore! She always wanted to be a writer but was persuaded by her husband (who was very competitive and a writer himself) to pursue a more practical path. He thought she should just settle down, get a secure paying job, and not bother with such selfish pursuits. Great advice, huh? Well five years later, she's getting the financing for her first comedic screenplay after running a major network development department and writing numerous insightful and humorous pieces for magazines and newspaper. I'd say her courage has paid off in spades. Hell, we even wrote a sitcom together and not only was it really funny, but we had a blast doing it. She totally reconnected with the spark that made her feel connected to who she was and the result is, she's back—stronger, funnier, and better than ever. I thought she was funny in eighth grade, but if the truth be told, she's even funnier now.

For me, it was my writing. I was an English major at McGill University and since I was a child, I've loved to write in my journal and read as many books as I can get my hands on. Having a creative outlet was a lifeline during my divorce and turned into a job afterward. As a matter of fact, most women I know who get through the divorce cruise intact have managed to connect with something in themselves that they actually enjoy doing. And you know what? A substantial number of them have even translated their passions into a career. Imagine that! What makes us unique, but that we are sometimes too frightened to explore, can actually be our salvation in the end.

The opportunity can present itself in a million different ways if you're open to it. For me, it was in a dear friend who I have had a working relationship with for thirteen years. Sometimes we're up—a hit show, travel, product endorsement, career longevity—and sometimes it's down (countersuing each other, not speaking, and general ongoing hostility). But when the chips were down and I had just arrived back in Canada after my messy divorce, we reconnected in a big way. He got a great offer to do a morning radio show on a new station and he said he wouldn't do it unless I came along for the ride. A couple of meetings later I not only had a job, but was having more fun than I could possibly imagine, even if I did have to get up at 4:30 in the morning.

In fact, we recently filmed another season of our show *He Said, She Said with Ken and Mary Jo.* I guess you could say it's a hit. And our friendship is for life—he is part of my family.

How can this all work for you? The first thing you should do is pretend you are talking to your daughter or a beloved friend who has been through a hard time. If you sat this person down, what would you tell her? To live in fear under the radar and always settle for less? Hell no! You would tell her that her salvation lies in her hard-earned ability to choose and to choose well.

How about starting small? Look at an old picture. What do you see and what sort of memories and feeling does that bring back? Maybe your daughter used to love to play chess but gave it up because it was considered geeky. But maybe it made her feel really good. And what about your friend?

Remember how she used to love to cook and try new dishes but her husband always put her down so she gave that up too? We all have to start somewhere, no matter how small, to put back the pieces that once comprised our lives. And that is how you do it: one step and one decision at a time.

Unless I had taken the time and energy to reconnect with the things in my life that made me feel, well, like me, I would probably be sitting around in a padded room right now, lovingly scrapbooking my favorite divorce depositions in a leather-bound book, simply titled *My Year of Living Hell*. Unfortunately, though, there's no time for that now. I have a job to do, a potential date to live for (no exact timeline on that one), and there is still tremendous fun to be had. I have a feeling if I just keep checking in with that girl I used to know and like, this second act is going to be one hell of a ride!

chapter 7

back on the market

Doesn't the phrase "back on the market" feel like a supermarket analogy? It's like we're past an acceptable expiration date and back in the used-goods section of life. On the market we go: to rot and ferment alongside the ripe and firm cantaloupes that are fondled and admired all day long by those looking for a sure thing.

But weren't we once a sure thing? Just because we've been placed back on the supermarket shelf of life doesn't mean our goods aren't good enough. We're not just an item being returned at a discounted price. In fact, we're worth more because of all we've experienced and have to offer. From now on, "back on the market" means "back by popular demand!" Like a hit Broadway show that has added extra performances to satisfy all the frenzied fans. And that's exactly what we're going to do: allow all those who missed out the first time round the opportunity to experience us now. How lucky are they?

And how lucky are we? Okay, I can hear some of you saying that the whole reason you got married in the first place is to never hear your name and "single" in the same sentence ever again. And I know there is a possibility that being single again is your worst nightmare come true. But if you're being honest with yourself, your divorce probably has the top spot here, so enjoy the fact that things could be worse!

Hey, you could still be married to the man who sold your mother's wedding dress on eBay and then charged you for shipping in his settlement request. Being single is not the end of the world. It's the beginning of the next chapter in your life. I hate to tell you this, but I actually know living, breathing women who love being single. You couldn't pay them enough to put up with a man. There are real benefits to letting loose and enjoying yourself with a man (or men) after being with just one for so long. Birds do it. Bees do it. Hey, men do it. So why can't unattached women do it too? Now go out there and have some fun!

It really is time to embrace and accept that at some future date, near or far, we are going to experience the charms of another man. We will preen and wax ourselves into a stupor for the chance, big or small (no pun intended), that a male we desire will desire us in return. The need to be appreciated is human nature. And as much as I deny it and fight it at every turn, men are here not just to divorce and despise. They can actually be fun, smart, and sexy and not at all creepy and moronic.

Think back to the time when a better part of your waking hours involved men—the target, the chase, the capture. Remember when it was a good thing to be taken by a man? Back when "being taken" meant giving into your vulnerable side and laying your emotions bare? It had nothing to do with having your shopping records subpoenaed. You were confident in the fact that if you gave in and fell, you would perhaps get screwed, but in the best possible of ways. But right now, you're like a mini-fortress with your drawbridge tightly closed, feeling a little too empathetic toward Queen Elizabeth the First—the virgin queen.

Let's face it, right about now you probably need a little havoc and pillaging in your medieval village and if you have any intention of lowering that bridge, it is time to get back on the proverbial horse.

The Changing Landscape of the Dating World

I remember in eighth grade when dating meant someone asking you to "go around" with him after school by the mall fountain. You sealed the deal with a doughnut and a commitment to meet tomorrow at the same time, by the same fountain, but perhaps with a different doughnut selection. It was pretty straightforward. You would then break up a few months later, cry as you walked alone by "your" fountain, and eventually move on.

There was a cyclical feel to it—a different grade, a new school, or another location would magically produce the opportunity for another boyfriend to appear. Now, I did notice the closer I got to thirty, the less likely it became that those boyfriends would magically appear. As a matter of fact, I remember being at my married, younger sister's house for Easter dinner with all of my siblings and their partners, and being told that the last single holdout, my friend Sue, had just "hooked one." My family gently reminded me that I was indeed exiting my twenties and perhaps the time had come for a bit of a fire sale. I was still youngish, but let's face it, entering the dark side.

I remember getting up from the table, feeling the need to get some fresh air. On the way out, I accidentally closed the door on my hand. I felt terrible—in part because of my hand, but more so because I was the only single one left. How had this happened to me?

I decided to start being more proactive. I rearranged the hours at my job. Working nights as a chef wasn't helping my single status. That ought to do it, I thought. And it did! I met my ex-husband a week later and within one year we were married. Side note: I wonder if I jumped the gun on that one. Any women out there who got married in one year or less, find a water cooler and discuss.

Back to the topic at hand. Now that we're divorced, things are a bit different when it comes to dating. Okay, a whole lot different. We're older, a little gun shy, and a bit out of the dating loop. We need to use the resources that are available to us to get back into that dating. I have two words for you, ladies: online dating.

Electronic Hookups

Perhaps you are already familiar with the joys and woes of online dating. Maybe you met your ex online. Or maybe you're not as familiar. The world of cyber-dating has become the local bar of the twenty-first century, except without the alcohol, the human contact, or the bowl of peanuts. Our online profiles sum us up in a paragraph and our Photo-shopped pictures present all of our dating virtues to anyone with electronic access who's interested. Within ten minutes, if you are willing and slightly computer savvy, you can be arranging dates, e-mailing dozens of potential suitors, and entering chatrooms that will explore your most intimate desires. Sure beats the fountain and doughnut hookup by a mile. Or does it? What about the personal touch? Does wanting that make us out of touch?

Many people will be eager to tell you about the benefits of Internet dating. They'll regale you with stories of people who hooked up with doctors, lawyers, investment bankers, and fabulous partners all through synching up with someone online. Believe it or not, it actually does happen. And the best part is, there's an online dating site for everyone. What do you fancy: a millionaire, a boy toy, a single dad, a farmer, a nudist, a conservative, or a sex partner? It's like ordering from IKEA with the potential for a booty call before they put your furniture together. If you can think it, you can find it online. Overwhelmed? Don't be. Let's break it all down and consider the pros and cons of dating—both electronically and personally.

The online hookup is really how most people seem to be, well, hooking up. I have tried it myself. I had a nonexistent dating life and friends were teasing me for my apparent inability to even secure a date. So one day when I couldn't take it any longer, I signed up. I signed up for all the sites: Singleparents, Lavalife, JDate, womenontheverge, liberalsforlove, BlackSingles (they recruited me: who was I to turn them down?), widowsrus, and various other opportunities. My monikers were FunInTheMorning (after the name of my radio show for the career-driven sites), DirtyGirl69 for Lavalife (wanted to seem open), and OlderbutStillFlexible for the "cougar" appeal I was

sure to have, being over forty and all. I tried to cover all my
bases. As I soon learned, apparently, everyone else was doing
the same thing.

At first, I couldn't keep up with all the flirts and e-mails
in my box. Was I really that popular or was it just part of
being the new gal in town? Whatever it was, my dating life
was taking up an alarming amount of my time, despite the
fact that I had not actually been on a single date. I was starting to become addicted to the adrenaline rush of flirting in
cyberspace. I became brazen and wanton in my correspon-
dence, but the thought of actually meeting someone was
terrifying. And the closer I was getting to a date, the more
isolated I was beginning to feel. Throw in the fear of telling someone my real name and run the risk of having him
Google me, and I was totally paralyzed.

You may think I sound paranoid about the Google
thing, but it actually happened several times. I even
had one person write me a five page e-mail telling me
how unimpressed he was with my "fame" (huh?), that he
knew people way more impressive than me, and that he
would not be used as a guinea pig in my search to exploit
innocent bystanders. According to him, I was pathetic,
manipulative, and would probably tip off the paparazzi
about our date. However, if forced, he would meet for
drinks, providing I pay. Another fellow who called himself "the king of hot tubs" in Southern Ontario called me
a turkey for not accepting his offer to go to Niagara Falls
for the weekend. He said I was "just like the rest of them"
who didn't realize how wonderful he was—just a big old
turkey. I also had a marriage proposal from a man who
lived in a truck with seven kids.

But (and there is a "but" here) I actually did meet some-one online. And I liked him, quite a lot actually. We saw each other for about a month. And you know what? I really enjoyed it. Confident that I wasn't a total train wreck and that someone found me acceptably attractive, I started to look at the universe very differently. I began to notice that there actually were some nice men around and maybe it was like a radio frequency—unless I was tuned in, I wouldn't get the station. What's the point of being open to a new and exciting signal if you are not dialed in?

I would like to be able to say that we merged our fami-lies, moved in together, and bought a rambling old house with three fireplaces and a huge kitchen, but truth is he dumped me via e-mail. Apparently, he was on the verge of making a commitment and resented me for it. It seems for-tyish with two young kids wasn't so hot . . . for him. But I don't regret it. We had a blast and I had dates and some-thing to talk to my friends about for at least six months. It was so worth it. Also I did a spectacular payback—but I'll get to that later.

> "I met my future husband online.
> After twenty-seven bad dates and a
> bout of carpal tunnel syndrome, I'm finally in
> love. Who knew your computer could be your
> highway to love and happiness."
> ~Heather

The point is, online dating is a great way to get back in the game. But be warned, it is addictive. You'll also find yourself becoming attached to people who have e-mailed you once, imagining your second wedding (in the Caribbean, naturally), and the trips and dinners you will have together. Be careful, though; you can start to take things very personally. You can also see when you log in if the person you are cyber-stalking is online as well. It can be very disillusioning to see the man you have fallen in love with on the Internet 24-7, especially when it's not with you. Even though the computer is a buffer, it can feel very real and confusing when you're trying to get back on the dating horse, so to speak. Getting rejected in cyberspace is like getting rejected in person. It just sucks. But hey, that's a part of dating and life in general and that's what you're doing right now—living your life. Have a little fun online. Create a fabulous profile, pick a site (any site), and knock yourself out. You know what they say: what happens online, stays online. Sounds good to me.

The Old-Fashioned Way:
Fix-ups, Blind Dates, and Booty Calls

Of course, the flip side of looking for love electronically is to look for it face-to-face, or at least with the help of another human. After you get divorced, it seems that every friend, family member, and business associate magically has that "perfect someone" they want to set you up with—and it's going to be the hookup of the century! People want to help you find love and be happy and (perhaps more importantly) they want to be responsible for it. So it's not a terrible thing to take them up on their offer.

Be prepared that if you decide to go this route, the "perfect someone" may not be so perfect after all. Case in point: the wonderfully charming guy my sister set me up with. He was a photographer and was bright, funny, and adorable. We met for dinner and I was having a great time. After the meal, he said he wanted to start hanging out with me on a regular basis. Before I could respond, he told me he had just moved in with his girlfriend and would I like to have dinner with them Sunday night? It was a potluck and they didn't have dining room chairs but who cares? They were used to "doing it on the floor" (dinner, he meant). Was I free? I left and called my sister.

Blind dates aren't always that bad (some can be even worse!). But every so often, the heavens open up, the angels start to sing, and a setup can actually work—especially if the person who set you up knows and loves you and actually thought this match through. There's even the possibility that you might actually have things in common and may have an enjoyable time. It might not be love at first sight. In fact, you may want to give that fight or flight response a chance to settle down before you bolt at the first red flag. And even if things don't go perfectly, a second date is always a good idea. You tend to be a little calmer, a tad more objective, and maybe a bit more open after your initial terror has subsided somewhat. After a dicey first date, I fell for one of my favorite boyfriends during date number two.

Overall, you have nothing to lose. Get out there and give yourself a chance. Hell, give your friends a chance too. You get the opportunity to meet new people, feel human, get dressed up, and be connected. It's a reminder that those in your life really care about your well-being. They're probably nervous setting you up after all you have been through, but they do it because they care. You should care, too. It's all part of getting the real estate that was your life out of foreclosure. It's time to renegotiate your mortgage, one banker at a time. Preferably while looking hot and slightly bothered.

Now on to booty calls. I personally feel there's absolutely nothing wrong with them—as long as your children aren't home and are in no way compromised. In fact, booty calls can be extremely fun. It's a physical encounter with someone you barely know, predicated on your attraction to each other and nothing else. I don't think that is a bad thing if you can handle it for what it is—a physical merger with no emotional commitment attached. If you are comfortable hitting the social scene and scoping out potential possibilities, you should give it a try. It could be something you really enjoy and it might give your old morale a little boost. Booty calls are a right of passage that man have been enjoying for years—it might be time to share the wealth.

Here's where my theory comes in to play. If going out to a bar or a party and hooking up with a man just for some physical intimacy is not even a possibility for you, then why can't we shop around for the perfect little black dress of the dating world?

Hear me out. I think it's really important for women to get "back on the saddle." Men have no problem climbing back up there. We, on the other hand, tend to stay planted on the ground. Our problem is separating sex from a relationship, and we find it hard to have one without the other.

What happens is that we go a long time without both—kind of like never using your wedding china or your living room until there is a special occasion.

"I thought booty calls were a hip-hop move or perhaps an aggressive shoe sale. Who knew that women could set up appointments for, um, physical pleasure? Have you heard of anything better?"

~Laila

Many women need help in this area and are too scared to take things into their own hands out in the real world. How great would it be if there were somewhere we could go where we would be "taken care of" so to speak? You know, a hot, caring man to coax us into the new millennium of our lives. A master teacher who excels in touching the depths of a woman's soul, enlightening and igniting her inner thoughts and nuances, who is sensitive to the affects of a lunar eclipse on our hearts and minds. We need someone who can boost our self-confidence and send us on our way with a spring in our step and a smile on our face. What I'm talking about sounds a lot like a male escort, but a booty call would do just fine here. And if they teach us a few of the new techniques that can help us out there in the dating world, hey, that's a bonus.

So, What Exactly Is Your Type?

If you spend enough time thinking about it, you might get
confused if you try to answer this question. As I said in the
online dating section, it seems like there is something out
there for everyone and quite truthfully, a lot of people seem
to give most anything a go. And I guess the $64,000 ques-
tion is, should you?

Now, don't forget, you've acquired an arsenal of dating knowledge here: the online thing, blind dates, friends
hooking you up, and the occasional booty call. So you actually have the resources to draw upon if you're really serious
about this getting on with your life thing. As a matter of
fact, as I write this, it's Wednesday. I know in and of itself
that doesn't seem that interesting. But what if I told you
that on Sunday I was so sick and tired of my complete lack
of a dating life that I went to my computer, found a good
dating site, and signed up, baby! And you know what?
Not only have I been having fun playing around online,
but I also have date on Friday—with a man! Yes, an actual
man. He's older, seems accomplished, and appears to be
quite pleasant. Last time, I married a hot guy and look
what that got me.

I've decided to take a whole new approach to dating and
allow myself to experience the nuances that different men
have to offer. The most important thing here is that if I had
not decided to take some action, I would be home watching
SpongeBob SquarePants with my daughter this Friday, wondering how it was possible to have so much hate for such a
little yellow sponge. I took this as a sign that I desperately
needed some adult time, and I bet you do too!

So what's your type now—post your divorce and all? Should he be young and hot, or older and settled? Is he sporty, serious, short, or tall? Is money more important then looks or do you have your heart set on a boy toy just for the physical thrill of it all? Do you want a companion with the potential for a long-term partnership or an in-and-out (no pun intended) rogue who is free to come and go as he pleases (again, no pun intended)? Have you thought about this before or have you always just gone with the flow? If the latter is the case, maybe it's not such a bad idea to put a bit of thought into this equation. Remember, we just unloaded someone who so did not work for us, so tailoring our "order" this time around might not be such a bad thing. For example, when I was in the thick of my foray into online dating, I found there were a lot of hot, young men who wanted to be with an older, more sophisticated woman. (Guess what, ladies? They find us hot. Thank you, Demi!) I was attracting kids (I mean, men) as young as twenty-two. And believe me, they were up for it—in every way.

Now for me, I just couldn't do it. I kind of felt like their mother. Mind you, a mother who had them at thirteen, but still too much of an authority figure for that type of connection. But I had friends who jumped in with both feet and were definitely enjoying the charms and advantages of dating a younger man. They were passing on the mutton and going for the lamb. They had no interest in an equal or someone older—they wanted lovely looking, younger men with no complications and/or similarities to their ex-husbands. Of course, in the end, everything gets a little complicated and messy, but for my gals, they never wavered. They wanted hot and they got it!

The Top Ten Problems with Dating a Younger Man:

1. He picks you up for your date on his skateboard.
2. He calls you "Mommy" at inopportune times.
3. You go out for lunch and he orders peanut butter and jelly.
4. You constantly have to tell him to turn the radio down.
5. When he says things like, "OMG, ATAB" you have no idea what the hell he's talking about.
6. You feel horrible when you inadvertently tell him that there is no Santa Claus.
7. After you make love, he asks for a juice box
8. His final exams coincide with your first day of menopause.
9. After dinner, he'll ask if he's eaten enough to get dessert.
10. He won't know the first thing about female genitalia.

The Top Ten Problems with Dating Older Men:

1. He's overly concerned with staying regular.
2. You're always walking a fine line between getting him excited, but not so much that he could suddenly die.
3. He talks about his favorite war.
4. Sure, he makes a good living, but by the time he pays for two alimonies, child support, and his Viagra prescription that Medicare doesn't cover, his idea of fine dining is the "Two for $20" deal at Applebee's.

5. He kindly tells you he can't see any wrinkles on your face but what he fails to mention is that, with his cataracts, he can't see much of anything.
6. You're unnerved whenever he calls you, "Baby" because frankly, he's old enough to be your father.
7. He has a rotary phone and a VHS player.
8. It's hard to be casual when he has a four-hour erection with your name written all over it.
9. You and his daughter were BFFs in high school.
10. He won't know the first thing about female genitalia.

I found the opposite was true as well. There were women who had been so badly bounced around in their marriages and their divorces that all they wanted was security, kindness, and stability. And as nice as a twenty-year-old can be, he probably still lives in his mom's basement. These women want, and are looking for, an older man—someone confident, adoring, and established in their life. For me, ninety-years-old, a billionaire, and terminal is a good combo, too. It just depends on what you're looking for.

It's always good to be flexible (especially when dating younger men), and realize that right now you don't really owe anybody anything. So if you have always wanted to slip into a different world, now's a good time to slip. Let's face the fact that some of us became a little complacent in our marriages and we might have even picked someone specifically so we could do that. Well, now is the time to actually try a whole lot of different appetizers—or, go right to the dessert if you want. You can date an artist, a yoga teacher, or a gynecologist (always wondered about this one)—it's up to you. And during this time when you're restructuring your life, you might be very surprised about what will make a perfect fit. And when you least expect it, that disheveled English professor with the liquid brown eyes (and no money, sadly) could sneak right up on you.

Red Flag Warnings!

"Red sky at night, sailor's delight. Red sky in the morning, sailors take warning." See how easy those nautical people have made it for themselves? They're smart enough to know that this simple and accurate credo is the key to keeping them out of harm's way. Doesn't it kind of make you wish you were a sailor? Wouldn't it be a relief to be able to recognize the turbulent waters and stay far, far away from those riptides that tend to pull us all under? To learn how to navigate the choppy seas of our rebirth and keep ourselves buoyant as we approach the virgin territory of our new land alert, aware, and armed with a revised and effective survival manual?

What I am trying to say with the water analogy is: how do we pick a winner this time around? Somebody who doesn't hit on your sister, mother, your brother, or best friend? Someone who can go to the bank for you without committing identity theft? Somebody who enjoys your company and never considers the possibility of your untimely death from a macadamia allergy and the ensuing funds that will follow? How do you find someone who wants you for you and isn't preying on your slightly vulnerable state of mind post-divorce? And God forbid, how do you protect yourself from hooking up with the exact same personality type that just about did you in first time? You have to look for the signs. As the saying goes, "seek and ye shall find." People are always, in one way or another, telling you exactly who they are. The key is to read the signs.

Exclusions worth noting at this time are your garden variety sociopaths and psychopaths. At this juncture, some general research on social outcasts would be helpful. It's always good to be aware of what makes a "great narcissist" and a "social deviant"—you know, for future reference. However, that's way beyond the scope of this book. Barring some pretty nasty psychological disorders, here are some of the signs that you might want to keep looking before you start planning your second marriage (and subsequent divorce):

Top 10 Red Flags for New Relationships

1. He can't remember his address.
2. He lives with your ex-husband.
3. He likes to practice your signature—"for fun."
4. He has a license plate collection in the trunk of his car.
5. He has been married five times.
6. And widowed five times. Talk to his parole officer.
7. There is nothing he won't do for you, if he is paid.
8. He claims his Internet porn addiction is just to sharpen his computer skills.
9. He starts drinking at 10:00 A.M. because, as he puts it, every day with you is a celebration!

And the biggest Red Flag that something might be a little dicey with your new beau . . .

10. He's dating your brother.

As you can see, if you're open to giving your dating life a try, you have to be very selective during the screening process. Dating and hooking up is great, but not when it is to the detriment of our health and well-being. Don't we all have those friends who talk about the trials and tribulations of their relationships with excruciating minutia but never change things an iota? What's worse, besides the hours of your life that you will never get back, if they finally do manage to extricate themselves from the situation, they proceed to find the exact same type of guy who does exactly the same type of thing. And you get to hear about it all over again! It's almost like getting to relive your crappy marriage on a daily basis. It almost always goes something like this:

Crazy Friend: I know, I know, he's a little undependable but his first wife emotionally abused him and he's practicing withholding his affection to rebuild his broken trust mechanisms. He loves me, almost too much really, and it's getting in the way of him breaking his insensitive and demeaning treatment of me and my feelings. And I know very soon I will get to see where he lives, it is just the renovations took a little longer then he expected and he doesn't want me to see everything until it's perfect. Plus, he is just in the process of evicting his ex-girlfriend from the premises. Can you believe her? The nerve. What is she, a squatter or something? And hey, what's another two years? When you're committed—

it's nothing. Though I am just a little concerned about one thing. . . .

Here is where you interject. Concerned at this point for her mental well-being and hoping beyond hope that there might be some acknowledgment of the field of red flags she's been ignoring you give it your absolute best shot.

You: Look, I just want to let you know that I am here for you. And good for you for being honest with yourself. You know this whole situation has been a little toxic and time consuming (for both of us) and I am so proud you're taking back the power and changing the dynamic of your life. You are . . .

At this point she interjects, looking lost and slightly terrified.

Crazy Friend: I'm worried about that kitchen he is renovating—what if I don't like it? And what if he doesn't have stainless steel appliances and proper counter space? What if he goes for faux wood paneling? How can I possibly sleep at night knowing that the first thing I'll have to do after becoming his wife (fourth to be specific) is to re-renovate the kitchen? I hate him for doing this to me!

And so it goes. And so will your mental health. So please feel free to use other people's mistakes to help you recognize the potential ones you want to avoid. Looking at others in your life who tend to ignore the warning signs that precipitate their own tsunamis is a good exercise. You can actually learn something from being present in your own life and observing what goes on around you. Think of it as free therapeutic advice—life really can be a giant doctor's office if you let it. And seriously, what would you rather spend your time on? Avoiding some of the basic mistakes that got you into this divorce mess to begin with, or trying to get your house out of foreclosure thanks to your new "real estate mogul" boyfriend? We have got to start paying attention to the signs.

Dating with Children

Internet dating, hookups, blind dates, and the odd booty call—how does this cornucopia of dating delights mesh with your role as a mom and caregiver to your kids? It all comes down to this: You can have the time of your life right now. After all, you are a consenting adult and chances are you have been through hell, but your kids don't need to know anything about it.

For some of us, this "throwing our dates in the kids' faces" thing might just be one of our major issues with our exes. Some of them may have taken the relationship equivalent of a packet of Tang, added water, and created an instant family. He might already have a new girlfriend, perhaps who lives with him, and maybe even with kids of her own. Or, worse, your ex may have a live-in who wants to have a New Year's baby and you just happen to notice it's already Memorial Day!

Things can move really quickly when people get out of a relationship. And how can we expect our children to grieve and understand the loss of their own family as they know it if Mommy or Daddy already has a brand-new partner or family in place? The message it sends to them is: "You were a really good family while it lasted but I think I hooked a real winner this time round. And don't worry, it might seem like I just met your new mommy, but we have been together for ages—just ask your mom! And wait until you meet her kids! I mean, your new brothers and sisters! We're like the best family ever, minus your mom and your own bedrooms, because now you have to share. Anybody want to go to Disneyland?"

Sadly, as so many of us know, that is not even an exaggeration. It happens all the time. Hey, it happened to my family. The new woman was introduced to the kids within a few weeks—against professional counsel—and it made things hell. The rule of thumb is to wait a minimum of six months, or even better, a year, to make the introductions. Take care of your first family first! Build up trust and establish the new dynamics of your reconfigured family. Make it about the kids and not about your ego. And when things start to settle and people begin to heal a little, then make the transition slowly and thoughtfully. It's not a fire sale. Not everything is replaceable. You can't swap item A for item B and think that nobody will notice. Your family is your own little piece of this world and at its core reflects who and what you are. Treat it with respect and dignity and give it the time it needs to mend in a real and meaningful way.

You're a Parent, Not a Leper

Now, on to how you can get lucky in a real and meaningful way, and still have the kids around. It is so doable—and so are you! Assuming that enough time has gone by and they're ready, most of the time it's fine for your kids to see that you're enjoying your life even though Daddy is no longer in the picture. It says that you have moved on and that life does not end just because your marriage did. Why can't you go out and have fun with friends and, God forbid, maybe even go on a date?

My ten-year-old son makes fun of me constantly for my lack of a dating life. He even wrote in the dust that collected on my car window, "My mom needs a boyfriend—apply here." I was proud not only because he spelled everything correctly, but also because he wants me to be happy and content in my new skin. The last thing kids need is to see us hurt or devastated by another man. So before we bring one home, let's make sure he's a keeper!

Logistically, it's a bit tricky to be having a dating life when kids are around, but planning ahead can make all the difference. Plus, all the sneaking around is kind of hot! Utilize the time when your ex has the kids. You have every right to use your home for entertaining when the children aren't around. And speaking of kids, make the house seem like they aren't around either. Don't be misleading about your life, but at least hide the car seat. Take SpongeBob out of the video player, serve cheese and crackers instead of chicken nuggets, and designate an adult area where you can at best feel psychologically a little separate from the kids. Get an arsenal of good babysitters and meet in bars and restaurants. Enjoy your dates and just accept that for right now, you are living a bit of a dual life.

Keep in mind that some people would kill to be living any other life then the one they are living right now. You will have your "mom" hat and your "hot crazed dating lady" hat. And at one point, the two will meet. But for right now, keep them separate and distinct. If you have kept the

family intact and are starting to have a real and viable dating life, then you're beginning to have it all. Imagine soccer
and family time on Monday night, and making out in your
boyfriend's car on Tuesday afternoon. And don't worry about
the kids. Your ex-husband is taking care of them while your
guy is taking care of you. Live a little. After all, how satisfy-
ing is it to be a little dangerous on a Tuesday afternoon, and
still being a great, kick ass mom?

chapter 8

rules of engagement

Let's face it. For most of us who have been enjoying the perks (not) of the never-ending divorce cruise, the universe feels pretty lawless. A *Lord of the Flies* for adults if you will. We have been slugging it out in the most primitive of ways, fighting for our basic survival against heathens (lawyers) and trollops (new girlfriends). The civilities of life as we know it have vanished and we've been engaging merely to sustain. If a good day is a visit to your lawyer's office for companionship and free photo-copying, then you're hurting. And not only are you hurt-ing, but you have lost all perspective. Life can be good, and there are people out there who live to a higher stan-dard. And that can be you—really!

Right now, we're clearly in the rebuilding portion part of our program. Our divorces are filed all cozy and comfy, we more or less know the terms of our arrangement (give or take a paragraph or two), and the once-married girl is now a single, liberated woman who is taking charge of her own life. Wouldn't now seem an opportune time to not screw it up again? Shouldn't we take a slightly different approach to our mental and emotional well-being and be involved—just a little?

We've been handed a great gift and we've got to grab it. And to grab life by the balls, we have to believe that we deserve the experience of actually getting what we want, and that we're more than worth it. Your past mistakes teach you what you don't want and hopefully guide you toward what you do. Our divorces have afforded us the chance to actually stop, take inventory, and have a second shot at getting it right. Come on—that is a tremendous thing! If you don't quite see it this way, think about your neighbor, your friend, or a relative who is unhappily married. Just think: as you're figuring out how to achieve your full potential in life, he or she is probably getting chastised for buying the wrong type of lunchmeat. Count your blessings!

Now is the time to throw a little caution to the wind and to just jump in. When it comes to dating, don't sit around waiting for a big old sign that says you're ready to get into a relationship again, because it just won't happen. For me, the trauma of my divorce, as I am sure for you, has been paralyzing. I think a personal low was when my ex-husband got remarried almost six months to the day after he filed for divorce. I was at the corner store getting some juice for my kids when I saw photos of their wedding splashed across a magazine cover. Against my better judgment, I opened up the magazine and there it all was. All splayed out for my enjoyment. A private ceremony, except for a magazine photographer, a lighting crew, and an additional film and sound crew to capture it for TV. There was a Fijian feast, pygmy servers, a lot of outfit changes, and frolicking and dancing in the sand. I was speechless as I flipped through the pages, but the best was saved for last. The article ended with my ex-husband quoted as saying something like, "I have never been more excited to make someone my wife than this one."

At this point, I was hoping he would fall on a pygmy server and the island of Fuji would sue him for manslaughter. But that did not happen. I bought my juice and the magazine and left. That was a hard day for me for all sorts of reasons. I was being sued, not by a pygmy, but by my daughter's birth father. It seemed all the publicity had not served my adoption well. But as you know, I won, and I haven't looked back since. And even though I have a lot of horrible memories in my divorce cruise scrapbook, I refuse to let it get in the way of the path I want to be on now. And that includes dating. True, there were no big signs that indicated I was ready to date, but eventually I knew in my heart that I was—no matter how painful my memories were. The path I want includes, and dare I say it, happiness, trust, and a relationship with a man who is worthy of the woman I was and have become.

What Makes a Relationship Work?

My first response to this question is probably the same as yours: "How the hell should I know?" My track record doesn't make me an expert, but I know it has afforded me the opportunity to talk to many men and women about this subject. And, no surprise, there seems to be a myriad of permutations on the formula since everyone is different. But regardless of the differences, the one common denominator seems to be that the two participants are on the same page about what's really important in life. They can be as dissimilar as the day is long, but their values (their mission statements, if you will) are simpatico. They might disagree on everything from politics to the weather, but at the core, they share a view of the world that includes and depends on each other. Youth, beauty, and sexual chemistry will all fade in and out, but if two people really want to be together, they will find a way— regardless of his hot and wanting secretary or her flexible and open yoga instructor.

No one is ever going to be perfect, but believe it or not, there are many couples who stay committed and focused on each other for the long haul. Actor Will Smith summed it up pretty well when, asked about marriage and divorce, he said, "Marriage is the most difficult thing you will do, ever. Divorce can't be an option—it's really that simple. You just remove the option because, if you have the option, one day that person's gonna make you wanna divorce." He wasn't advocating staying in a bad relationship. Rather, he was acknowledging the difficulty factor in maintaining a marriage and recognizing that the hard times are just built in and it is up to us to work through it responsibly to get to the reward on the other side. Imagine having to work at something to make it better. What a concept.

"I thought I was clueless on what makes a relationship work. But now I think it comes down to whatever happens, you know you'll be okay on your own. Men are wonderful, but so is your self-worth."

~Miranda

The question is: what makes a relationship work for you? In your marriage, were you the needy one who was just so grateful to be in a partnership that you didn't demand or expect anything from it? Was a good day flying under the radar, just thankful that he didn't you leave for someone better? Or did you expect too much and suffocate him with your insatiable appetite for more, meaning he could never measure up anyway? What was your role? Caregiver, mother figure, ice goddess, enabler, co-dependent, trophy wife, breadwinner, boss, or employee? How did you feel participating in your own relationship? Or maybe you weren't participating at all. Maybe you just felt nothing. And since you're divorced, chances are the role you had been cast in wasn't working for anyone. After all you have been through, what would be important criteria for a relationship to work?

You really need to get to the bottom of this one. For me, the most important requirements would be strength of character and dependability in a really hot package. He needs to be older this time round, established in his career, and understand the real nuances of life.

Now it's your turn. Make a list that illustrates what you think would work for you this time round—no matter how silly or weird. What would your top criteria be? Or perhaps, what would your bottom five, least desirable traits be? Have a little fun with it. Here's a list to get you started:

Top Ten Things That Make a Relationship Work
1. Hot monkey sex (hey, it's my list).
2. No Hawaiian shirts.
3. He calls you from work because guess what? He actually has a job!
4. He likes your friends—but not too much!
5. He loves your weaknesses more than your strengths.
6. He knows your coffee order.
7. He makes you smile, even when he's not around.
8. He appears to be the same person everyday.
9. He puts up the Christmas tree.

And the number one thing that makes a relationship work . . .

10. How the hell should I know? It's not important—as long as you know.

That's the truth. There is also some truth happening right outside your door, if you care to take a little look around. Believe it or not, maybe even within a twenty-mile radius of your own home, there are relationships that are working, thriving, growing, and flourishing. Can you imagine? Well, maybe you should start to. Not to get all secret on you, but the power of positive thinking and not giving into fear is life altering. You have paid your dues and if you have come through this experience with a little bit of faith and hope intact, then you have won. Now you can take those attributes that weren't stripped away and choose, yes, choose to create relationships that move and inspire you rather than paralyze and devastate you. You have that choice. So instead of mourning the silverware you lost in the divorce settlement, why not discover the gold in you that was left behind.

Pick Someone Worthy

You're now at the juncture where you'll really see how much you have learned from your past mistakes. As of late, the "relationship" portion of your life program has not really been the source of a whole lot of joy and happiness. In fact, it has been anything but. But hopefully, the fear of ever being in that position again will motivate you to make some brilliant and far-reaching choices. Because, guess what? You have options.

Of course, romance and hookups and relationships aren't just decided by the head; they have to have the cooperation of the heart. You can plan as much as you want, but before you know it, you can be in Las Vegas saying "I do" to someone who is a definite "I don't." The trick here is to have the insight and the self-esteem to gauge what is worthy of your time and your commitment. We have discussed red flags and huge warning signs and hopefully we now know the difference between an attentive boyfriend and one who should be institutionalized. We have to find a good balance here between the thrill of being alive and the lessons we have learned courtesy of our divorce cruise. All we have to do is look to ourselves to answer this question.

So, what does picking someone who is worthy mean? I think it goes back to being honest with your toughest critic: yourself. Looking back, there were lots of warning signs about my ex-husband and I totally and very consciously chose to ignore them. I really don't remember the first few years of our marriage very well, but I do recall being a bit disconnected. As a matter of fact, the other day my younger sister told me a story that I completely erased from my memory. One day, I called her very upset and wanted to meet for lunch. According to her, I was frustrated that I had absolutely nothing in common with my then husband and even having a conversation was a stretch. She basically said, "I told you so." How could I forget that? Talk about denial.

Looking back, I guess I always knew that after the years of mini-bombs, one day there would be a big fat Hiroshima. I just didn't know the Hiroshima would be Tori Spelling. How could I predict that? All I did know was that shortly after my ex left (nine days later to be exact) when he was giving interviews to the press, he confessed to watching reruns of *Beverly Hills, 90210* at home before hockey practice and admitted to having a crush on her. Apparently he had a lot spare time that I wasn't aware of. Sadly, the wife is always the last to know about these things. There is a lesson you can learn here, though. Take note of what your next boyfriend's television viewing patterns are. If you notice *Saved by the Bell* and *Love Boat* popping up on a frequent basis, you might have to start asking some tough questions!

Go with Your Gut

At this point when you're discovering that yes, you do have a boatload of great things to offer a partner, you might want to find a reliable harbor to park it. There are no guarantees in the relationship department, but you might want to consider trusting your gut. We women have a great ability to ignore things that make us uncomfortable or tell us that this particular situation is not a good one. We brush off the feeling, instantly thinking that we can make it all better. All we have to do is change that person. However, your divorce should really give you a heads up about this one: you can't!

Face it: you can't change anyone but yourself. So if you are starting this whole second act thinking all you have to do is submerge your real self to make the other person like you, you are screwed—and not in a good way. How can you have an authentic connection with anyone if you're trying to be what he needs you to be? What about you? What do you need to have a real and meaningful and healthy partnership?

Yes, we're back at that honesty thing again. So, be honest. If you find your new paramour is a little too aware of other women to the point of choking on a hamburger because he forgot to chew when a hot woman walked by (this happened to me—twice), you might want to address that. If he puts you down, laughs at your life plan, and measures your back fat, you might not have a stellar character on your hands. If his idea of a perfect night out is one without you, it could be a sign of bigger things to come. And if and when you happen to answer his cell phone the person on the other end asks for "Daddy" in a different language, then now might be the time to acknowledge you have a whole other set of issues to deal with.

Just be careful. And remember, if you really want to change the outcome, then change the rules and location of the game. If you want smart and successful, then don't join the junior high hip-hop team.

Join the museum, a gourmet club, take a Spanish class, go flamenco dancing—shake it up a little. If you want sporty, take your pick. I love football, so I joined a betting pool and it's been a blast. It may not be a huge romantic gold mine—my dad runs it and the other players are my kids and my Aunt Sue. But it helped rekindle my interest in football and got me into attending a game. I sat beside a really cute ex–football player and I let him explain the plays to me and then impressed him with my knowledge of the penalty system. I felt great afterwards. I also started going to special lectures and events at the art gallery in my hometown and met some wonderful characters through that venue. I even hosted a charity event for them where an eighty-four-year-old patron hit on me! He was kind of cute—in a George Burns kind of way. So, be smart and use the resources you have already put into place to hone in on what makes sense for you now—things that are worthy of your time and effort and that don't require a lawyer or homeland security. Say it until you start to believe it: "I am worthy, I am worthy, I am worthy. . . ."

I Feel, Therefore I Am a Loser?

Having a successful emotional life after divorce is one of my top challenges. How on earth can we ever feel safe enough to be "messy" with our feelings again if we've been made to feel less worthy because we have them? Isn't it good to be in touch with our inner workings so we can actually make life choices that reflect our place in the world? Isn't that what being authentic and human is all about? We know better than anyone where denial and disconnect can end up—in your lawyer's office, hysterically explaining why the leaf blower meant so much to you. It just seems if we don't have access to "us," then we don't have much of anything at all.

So now that you are ready to move forward into full-on life mode, how do you navigate this authentic emotional state without looking slightly insane? And if you're finally at the place of embracing your resurrected emotional state, how comfortable are you letting the genie out of that proverbial bottle? Or does it feel better and safer to just put a lid on it?

Don't you dare! After all the hard work you've done to get here, don't you dare revert back to your acquiescing self. Why the hell would you do that? You saw how well it worked for you the last time round and it sure wasn't a hit! Repressing your feelings and becoming disconnected is not really a good thing. In fact, it's a terrible thing and results in a blowup so out of proportion to the actual issue at the time that you become, well, just scary. It's also highly ineffective because by the time you actually express yourself, the truth behind the situation is gone. Even you probably forgot what the original instigator was. All you know now is that everything is just too overwhelming to face. In truth, this is what being in a bad marriage can feel like—a huge divide between what you meant and what you said, and you're stuck in the middle pleading, "I'm in here somewhere . . . help!" Right now, it's your job in the face of all this scariness to turn up the volume on that inner voice of yours and learn how to get people to listen to you without having to scream.

So let's start practicing, shall we? Let's take a little quiz (I love quizzes, especially when I know the answers). This is to prep you on handling being human again and opening yourself up to the universe without getting obliterated. Please answer the following questions honestly:

Question 1: Your boyfriend calls late and blows you off for dinner after you cooked for six hours and bought new dining room furniture. You feel taken for granted since this is the third time it has happened this week. Do you:

A. Call him and apologize, then find out where he is and drop off said dinner.
B. Say nothing, stand by the window, and hope he drives by.
C. Explain to him calmly and clearly that if it's that difficult for him to respect your time and efforts, then he would be better off purchasing a girlfriend online who is as obtuse and brain dead as he is. You are polite, though, and offer him a selection of helpful websites.

Question 2: You find two pairs of panties in his car that aren't yours and you suspect he might be straying. Do you:

A. Call him and apologize. Then, find out where he is and drop off said panties.
B. Say nothing, stand by the window, and try on said panties and hope he drives by.

C. Impound his car and change the locks on your door. Then, explain to him calmly and clearly that you will not tolerate dishonesty and disrespect and the fact that he felt compelled to cheat when he had such a wonderful woman is merely a testament to his complete and utter lack of character. Then hand back said panties.

Question 3: You finally have the courage to call up your boyfriend of six months to tell him how much you like him. You reach out, giving him a glimpse of your rich, emotional life. He responds by pretending his phone gets cut off, hangs up, and starts playing video games. Do you:

A. Text him and apologize, then go to the video store to get him Mortal Combat 7

B. Say nothing, stand by the window, and vow to never open up again.

C. Take it as a sign from God and tell him calmly and clearly he so failed your litmus test and please, don't let the door hit your ass on the way out! Amen and pass the ammunition!

"This time around I refused to compromise my feelings and emotions. And you know what? The man I'm with now loves my openness and vulnerabilities as well as my strengths. How great is that?"

~Kim

Let's recap here. In the quiz, we covered the big three, the holy trinity of relationships: respect, truth, and compassion. How did you do?

Please say you had a whole bunch of C's happening and that if you had an A or a B your pencil slipped. If you spent more than two minutes on this little test and you're feeling conflicted, I suggest either kicking your therapy up a notch or taking a break from the dating thing. It is time to match your emotions with real life. If you are upset and feel compromised and need to express that to the person you are with, you are not being difficult and therefore unlovable. You are being human and real and confronting the situation head on—perhaps something you did not do in your marriage.

By dealing with life as it happens instead of having your head buried in the sand, you are upping the ante on your own life. True, people might feel uncomfortable with the new you, someone who is resolute and taking the time to live purposefully. And you might lose some dead weight along the way. But in the end, you will figure out why someone is with you—and hopefully it is because of the whole package and not some cut-and-paste version of who they need you to be. Imagine the power and the potential in knowing who you are. Having a therapist tell you that: $250 an hour. Believing it yourself: priceless.

Keeping a Pulse in Your New Relationship

So, what's more terrifying right now: the thought of being alone for the rest of your life or actually moving forward and having a relationship with a man you love and who loves you back? Of course, there's danger in the second scenario. He could find out your secret flaws, have an affair with your best friend, or sell your house behind your back. Plus, he was probably sent here by aliens for some type of planned abduction, because no man on earth could ever want you again, correct? And really, when he finally figures out how damaged you are, you can forget the abduction—he'll just leave. Ladies, is this how you're thinking? Really? Just stop. This is our new beginning. If you're dedicated and hopeful and you've found a man who is really worthy of your love, then things are, or will be, exactly as they should be. You're in this new and wonderful place because of all the work you have done to get here. You're choosing life and happiness, and as we know from Chapter 5, there is no free ride on the happiness bus: you've got to work for it. If you're fortunate enough to have found the love you want, let's figure out how to make it the love you keep.

In this respect, our marriages hold some really good data if we care to take a look and learn. One of my best friends (recently divorced, by the way) had the most brilliant analogy regarding the state of marriage. She compared it to a bank and a ledger sheet. Every time you fight with your husband, go to bed angry, say hurtful things, don't sleep with him for a month, disagree about the kids, or look at him and wonder why the hell you married such an idiot, these things add up like a massive balance sheet outlining your debts and assets. And like a real balance sheet, it eventually resolves itself. The company can't stay afloat if what is owed overpowers what is left. Marriage and life are like that. At every juncture, every choice you make establishes unequivocally where you will end up. So if the choices you were making in your marriage were inauthentic at the core, it was only a matter of time before the whole damn company tanked. However, you get to do it differently this time round. Now, isn't that a relief?

Okay, so you've hooked a good one and despite being a little terrified and wobbly, you're moving full steam ahead. Have you thought about how you might want to do things differently this time around? Hopefully, you now understand the importance of being real and authentic in this union and not just a reasonable facsimile. So, if the mannequin lady is gone and you have stepped in, then now is the time to really commit to your man. That may have been hard to hear, but you need to say it to sell it. By now, you know that being committed isn't obliterating who you are for the sake of the relationship. On the contrary, it now means being fully present and active in your own life and your partnership. And the fact that you're brave enough to jump in again, armed with your hard-won experience and knowledge, is a definite strength and most certainly not a weakness. So keeping the bank and ledger analogy intact, how do we do it differently this time round? Accountability, plain and simple—you have to keep track of the emotional currency spent. You have to pay to play.

Kickin' a Little Ass

If you want a kick ass relationship, then you've got to kick some ass. You saw how standing on the sidelines did your marriage in. Do you want that game forever on instant replay? If you're really in love and excited by this relationship, then don't just leave it to chance. Take a chance and really try! Don't make it all about the kids every waking hour. Hopefully, your ex has the children at least part of the time, so you can use this break to enjoy your man. Don't be ashamed that you need alone time—dump your friends for a while, turn off the phone, and cancel your subscription to *Man Haters R Us*. Embrace the fact that you are once again part of a couple, but do it on your terms. Be conscious and aware of the climate of your life together. Of course, at the beginning all of this is easy and exciting as you bask in the early days of the honeymoon stage. But you know better than anyone this is not a permanent state of being. You've got to learn to shake it up to keep it up, so to speak.

And as we've discussed in this book, you're now CEO of your own company, and how you run it is up to you. Are you going to be the Microsoft of your generation or the Lehman Brothers? Do you want far-reaching initiatives as your corporate mantra or to just get the job done without breaking a sweat? And if you think of the last company and how it dissolved (divorce!) you'll want to implement some different strategies here.

First of all, don't be a victim. Take charge of your relationship with the same focus and tenacity you had while researching what it takes to drive someone clinically insane in ten days or less (with a money-back guarantee). If something feels wrong, fix it! Not patch it up, but actually fix it up. Communicate what your needs are and what you want. Don't be the Helen Keller of relationships. Let the other person in. We can do an awful lot of complaining and the whole "woe is me" thing is getting pretty lame. So whatever it takes to keep this new merger fresh and vital and profitable, do it!

I can't believe I'm quoting Dr. Phil again, but he did say one thing I thought was very true. Men, unlike woman, express themselves emotionally through physical intimacy and they need that connection to feel connected. In other words, the "sex thing" is pretty key to holding on to the "guy thing," unless otherwise agreed upon. Using our bank analogy, allot a really big fat column to this one, and monitor it on a daily basis. You will get away with a lot of miscellaneous withdrawals if you stay on top of the deposits. Make sure your balance sheet is clean on this one and make no mistake about it: if you carve out the time and energy for this column, your company will be turning a profit for years to come.

At the end of the day, it is not brain surgery: men and women are very different, but we still seek each other out for love and companionship even though historically we drive each other nuts. It probably boils down to a very basic formula: Man Unloading Dishwasher = Wife Having Sex with Him Frequently. It would all be so easy (or easier) if we just acknowledged the gaps and tried to close the divide . . . at least three or four times a week. Enough said.

Some Basic Guidelines for Round Two

Now would be a good time to regroup a little and see how far you have come in your post-divorce journey. If you're at the stage of being in another relationship with a human of the male persuasion and not wanting to kill yourself (or him), just look at how far you've come. Think back to when all this went down and the amount of devastation in your life. Did you ever think this wounded bird would come back stronger and more alive then ever? Well, you did, and now here you are! And if at this point there is no significant relationship going on, who cares? There will be soon, provided of course that you want one. Right now, priority number one is staying mentally healthy and open. And if there is a man involved in that equation we want it to be numerically correct on your scale of what is important. So along with all the other things you've learned (what makes a partnership work, finding someone worthy, and being emotionally authentic), you should make sure you have a few dependable basics in your relationship wardrobe. Like a great white shirt or a classic trench, we need the tools to build a complete and functioning wardrobe to embrace our new world and all it has to offer. You don't want to be committing the same fashion crimes you did when you were in the thick of your dissolving marriage. It is time to clean and fortify our emotional closets—say yes to some sexy black pumps and a definite no to pink track pants with "hot stuff" written on your behind. It's just common sense.

Now that you have your basic arsenal of things needed for said healthy relationship, you have to be ready to let go of it—if needed. Please don't go postal; just think about it. You have to be willing to bring up the uncomfortable stuff and what isn't working, and then even more importantly, implement things that could make it better. You're now armed with your post-divorce emotional wardrobe, so use it! Be honest and constructive and present. And if Mr. Wonderful just isn't wonderful enough, don't be frightened to get yourself out of a situation that has "Divorce Cruise,

Part Two" written all over it. Chalk it up to experience and move on with the attitude that you learned something from that situation that will help you in the next. It's all a part of our continuum.

Here are some other tips to keep in mind if you want to make this one last:

- Don't stalk anyone that you're dating or living with; it just sends a mixed message.
- Don't talk constantly about your ex-husband and his small . . . personality.
- In fact, keep your conversations with your new guy away from the intensely personal parts of your previous marriage and divorce. Dwelling on the minutia of your marriage and divorce could put someone off—permanently. There is a fine line between living in honesty and awareness and sounding like you are on the verge of Tourette's syndrome. Make it a point to learn the difference.

Now that you have this great second-act relationship, wouldn't it make sense to hold it to a different standard? Instead of trying to figure out a whole new emotional constitution, try using the code of ethics that have governed your best and most rewarding friendships. Usually, your friends like you just for you. They don't mind that you're slightly crazy or put the milk in the wrong area of the fridge. If you rant, they think it's entertaining and kind of cute. And when you're upset, they want to be there for you because you always are for them. Your honesty is refreshing, your life experience, an asset, not a deficit. In sum, you complete them! And all they seem to want from you in return is your company, respect, and love. They think on the friend level, you are one hell of a catch.

Imagine that! A relationship based on mutual admiration and respect. If you can get that, and the hot monkey sex, my work here is almost done. As a matter of fact, if you do find it, does he have a cousin? Just asking.

chapter 9

here you go again

Oh God, are we actually thinking of doing this again? Seriously? I think I might need a support group just to get this chapter out. I'll call it "The World of Remarriage and Our Place in It." There. I said it in a benign and hopeful way. Okay, here it goes.

If we want, we can choose to get married (again) to a man (voluntarily). Why we would ever put ourselves through that hell again is beyond me, but let's just acknowledge the option, shall we? We're not being forced at gunpoint or on the verge of being sold into a profitable slavery ring. We're consciously choosing a legally binding agreement with another man.

First reaction, adding to the sheer romance of it: check your 401(k) status and his criminal background. And while you're at it, what's an FBI trail to two people so in love? Diverting your funds to an offshore account and a quick sting to get his fingerprints? Still romantic but also smart. Who says you can't be in love and fiscally responsible at the same time? For me, that combo is actually foreplay!

But at this point, if you're happy and ready to commit to this institution one more time, how can I help but not get onboard? I know I've compared getting married to owning a cheese-producing cow (for profit) but I think after everything we've been through together, I'm softening, just a little. It might actually be nice to walk down that aisle again without the nagging feeling that we're throwing our lives away. Perhaps we really are wiser and happier with ourselves. And perhaps marriage, after all we've been through, is actually a good choice for us, and not a death sentence. How's that for positive thinking?

A Divorce Fairy Tale

The more I think about it, the more I'm starting to envision my eventual nuptials—on the coast of California, overlooking the Pacific Ocean on a cloudless day, surrounded by friends and family who bet the farm that I would never hook up again. I smile a little smugly as I drift down the aisle to join a man in a partnership I only dreamed about. He takes my hand and tilts my wrinkle-free face toward his.

I am like a young girl, innocent, wanting, and eager to start our life together as he introduces me to the wonders the world has to offer. I also make every effort possible not to imagine the impending earthquake that will surely happen. I will get tossed to sea, still in my wedding dress, as my grieving fiancé is consoled by my hot best friend. Six months later, I wash up ashore further down the coast to witness their wedding day with my father giving the bride away. I try to scream but a shark has eaten my tonsils and so it goes.

Okay, even though I might not be completely there yet, I did imagine myself in the dress.

Remarriage

All kidding aside, if you've arrived at the point where you're making this monumental decision without being drugged or threatened, then you really have overcome a lot of hurdles. To move forward in a binding relationship with a man you love and want to spend the rest of your life with is not only admirable, it is also brave. You must be feeling pretty good to take it all on again and really, at the heart of it, that's what this book is about: Being courageous enough to live and love your own life.

"I never thought I would get married again. My ex left me for my best friend when I was six months pregnant and took our bank account along with him. But here I am again because I believe in all of it: love, commitment, and happily ever after."

~Elizabeth

On the other end of the spectrum, if you're in a spectacular partnership and you would rather give birth to
triplets without meds than get married again, that's
okay, too. The happily-ever-after ending of a divorce
story doesn't have to be to remarry again. It's whatever
ending makes you happy. The only blueprint that you
have to follow now is the one that is right for you. And
if that blueprint includes getting hitched again, and all
that it entails, then you have earned your spot on the fun
and exciting (but not so exciting that you forget to keep
separate bank accounts) "remarriage cruise!" So, welcome
aboard—we've been expecting you!

Here you are with a ring on your finger and a man at
your side, ready to embark on the next phase of your adult
life. A "rebirth" if you will. To be able to go from a devastating divorce to the open arms of a new relationship with a
healthier game plan says a lot about the hard work and soul-
searching you have done (you have done it, right?). Making
sure that you've picked a good one and that you, as a willing
participant, have done your fair share of the work is crucial.
I'm just going to cut you a wide berth here and assume that
love has shown you the way and not the fear of ending up
like my Aunt Dot and Aunt Mad, two spinsters who shared
their golden years drinking beer, playing bridge, and eating
candy bars for dinner. Now for me, that really isn't the worst
scenario ever. On the contrary, I would rather have great
companionship and conversation (and candy bars) then be
in a lame-duck relationship where I feel miserable and alone.
So, in the spirit of love and conspiring with the universe for
wonderful gifts, it will be assumed that this union is worth
diving into all over again. You are . . . in love.

Dealing with the Haters

The time has come to really make the union public. Of course, getting married will accomplish that, but now is also the time to let your friends and family in on your new life plan.

Here's the catch: as elated and excited as you're feeling, that is also as judgmental and negative as some people will be. Major events in our lives bring out major reactions in our inner circle. Remember, throughout our whole divorce cruise, people reacted to our suffering, our pain, and even our successes. So their new reactions may not unnerve us as much now. But then again, they might.

Focus on your hard-earned happiness. What does anybody really ever know about your life, anyway? Providing you have chosen well, then all that's left to do is have faith. Faith in the fact that you know what the dark side has to offer and how it almost did you in a time or two. Faith in the fact that you fought for happiness and hope in your life and you have earned the right to choose what is best for you. And faith in the understanding that people's reactions often have way more to do with them than with you. So unless you really are marrying a serial killer or an actor (personal biases here), proceed directly to the wedding planner and just go for it!

In a way, you really have come full circle from where you started. From the day you knew you were going to get a divorce, to the time when you're planning your wedding. How's that for full-on resilience of the human spirit! Pretty impressive isn't it? And so are you. Just think back to a time when adult diapers seemed like a lifestyle option for extended bedtime, and personal grooming was for poodles and wimps. There was no spring in your step and the path ahead seemed pretty daunting and endless. How much value was there in that level of misery? But that was not going to be you—not for long. Being the driven type of gal that you are, you had no choice but to relocate. And having an eye for good real estate, you sold at the height of the market and took what you had accumulated and invested in something different—your future. You put your hard-earned currency in an up-and-coming area, not quite yet established, but bursting with endless potential, and decided to invest there. It was time to move from the old neighborhood anyway—there was nothing left of interest. As a matter of fact, that ship had sailed, and this time, that particular cruise was short one very important passenger: you. Seems you are a little too busy living your new life to be reliving your old one. Makes sense to me.

Hit Me Baby One More Time

It's a little weird isn't it? You might actually be at the point where you're planning your second wedding—perhaps some ten, fifteen, or twenty years after your first, becoming a bride one more time (and hopefully only one more time).

For many women, a second wedding can come to symbolize so much about their lives, where they are personally, and can even act as some sort of anecdote to their first set of nuptials. It's almost as if some second-time-around brides have to get it right by either completely removing the first wedding experience from their minds or making this one so over the top that just the tablecloths alone violate child labor laws in three countries. So, does wedding planning get any easier the second time round? From what I have heard, no. You're still crazy, out of control, and hypersensitive (kind of like your divorce, but instead, you're getting married). It's an emotional rain forest in which everything involved in your new marriage becomes intertwined with and reminds you of your previous marriage. There is no way you'll go through all of this without somehow having to address your first waltz down the old aisle. Don't panic; it's not at all bad. In fact, it can actually be healthy. Just like our support groups we sought out during our divorce, I think we should share our stories about wedding number one when we're gearing up for wedding number two. Clear the air so to speak, and gather the resources to tailor a day specific to how we want to express this new beginning in our lives.

I can't say that I'm engaged or even dating for that matter, but I know for a fact that I would do my second wedding a bit differently. I had a bit of a weird one the first time around. For starters, my parents were separated and hadn't spoken in a year. (Remember them? They inadvertently killed their therapist?) During that year, my father had hooked up with a younger woman whose career choice was teaching aerobics at the local YMCA. They were living together and apparently getting quite serious (unless of course her aerobic career took off and that could all change). At any rate, I only had three months to plan the wedding and very limited funding. So I turned to religion—specifically, my Aunt Sue.

My Aunt Sue is one of the most famous nuns ever and was awarded the Order of Canada by a representative for the Queen of England. She started an organization called "Out of the Cold" that fed and clothed homeless people in the freezing winter months, and she has been doing that for over twenty-five years. She is legendary in her tenacity and ability to get the job done. Also, at the time I got married, Aunt Sue and her fellow nuns lived in one of the most beautiful houses in Toronto, with a sprawling backyard that overlooked the city with terraced gardens. Because my budget was so minimal, the nuns offered me their fairy-tale mansion and I took it. But gorgeous setting aside, some strange things happened that day.

To begin with, I hadn't factored in the weather. It was 95 degrees outside and I had bought the most beautiful dress ever (on sale), but it was a winter gown. I think the heat stroke I suffered was the reason for the migraine that I got right after saying "I do." I headed back to the convent with my headache, about to call it a day and miss my whole wedding celebration, when one of the nuns pulled me into her room. She quietly slipped me some pills and not before or since have I ever felt so good. I didn't even mind that there was little to no food. We had planned an elegant cocktail reception with exquisite appetizers and drinks. Seems the food had arrived early and the nuns had been hungry . . . and you know how hard it is to control a pack of hungry nuns.

So, I had a reception where a majority of the guests were drunk (no food mixed with extreme heat and lots of iced cocktails can do that) and behaving quite inappropriately. To their credit, none of the nuns seemed shocked. As a matter of fact, they kicked up their heels, danced, and shared in the pizza I ordered later to keep the guests from becoming even more stinking drunk. Throw in two arrests (one due to disorderly conduct and the other to do with having sex in questionable areas of the convent) and my dad announcing his own wedding plans during the speeches, and it was a perfect day. A perfect day I might do a little differently the second time round.

Were you, or others, out of control your first time around? Was your day ruined because the centerpieces where a millimeter off and the water wasn't quite room temperature? Did you break down when your wedding song was cut short because your Uncle Walter face-planted into your maid of honor? Honestly—did you enjoy your wedding or was it all a crazy blur?

Maybe you didn't get your princess wedding that first time round either and this is your chance to fulfill all your childhood dreams. Or perhaps you have been there, done that, and nothing is more appealing than the thought of an intimate dinner and ceremony with your nearest and dearest.

What would have made your first wedding better and is there anything you can do in this bonus round to make it good for you? Oh yeah—and don't forget this time, you have a man who loves you and seems quite willing and able to take on a divorced woman and her family and the little bit of baggage she still carries round. That is really the best start you could hope for, because it sounds romantic and real all at the same time. And that's hot. It's even beginning to turn me around. I'm actually starting to think this whole remarriage thing might not be such a bad idea after all!

The Guest List: Exes, Stepkids, and Parents, Oh My!

Let's assume for good measure that you're moving forward on the type of wedding that you really want to have, be it big, small, catered, à la carte, or a just a BBQ and your fiancé. You have sorted through all the practical and emotional baggage to get to the heart of your wedding equation and it seems like everything is adding up. What would be perfect is if you just had to plan the party (pick a little food, a couple of flowers, and decide whether your father should give you away again—hey, maybe it's time to give your mother a shot).

It would all be good if that were the extent of your job. But alas, the bride also has another pretty major career objective here: the task of putting asses in the seats, so to speak. If you thought it was challenging to decide whether to wear white, ecru, or off-white, just wait until you have to comprise the actual guest list. Welcome to your very own version of *Apocalypse Now* as you navigate the jungles of your old and new life merging together as one. Talk about *Heart of Darkness*! Just wait until you have to do the seating chart.

It's easy for me to say that it's your party and you can cry if you want to, but there are a lot of players from a lot of different teams involved and you have to figure out which players you want to see in the finals. You've got your kids, family, and friends, plus his kids, family, and friends. And maybe some of those family and friends aren't too thrilled about this merger. You have to figure out who is going to make an appearance from your past life and who isn't. Also, which adorable child from which merging family is going to be the flower girl or in charge of holding onto the ring? And is their potential for some sort of walkout (a strike if you will) from said children who would rather support the Wall Street bailout (from their allowance) than support this union?

Please don't think any of this is easy or, on the other hand, foreshadows horrible things to come. Remember Carol Brady's wedding from *The Brady Bunch* when she and Mike merged six kids, two households, and a dog? It is worth noting that even though they came across as the perfect family, their actual wedding day was a disaster. The kids fought, the bride was cranky, and Mike and Carol ended up in the mud with their wedding cake splattered on their heads. But they all still moved on to be a really happy, close family—I think even a few of the kids dated each other. The fact is, your merger is a bit more complicated this time round. Both parties have prior assets, so to speak, that need to be assimilated into the company. And the wedding that you're now planning is the first major step in blending these two corporations together. And you thought you were just getting a ring on your finger!

So the question remains, who to invite and who to ignore? If your new man has kids, that's a no-brainer. Not only do you have to invite them, but it would also behoove you greatly to involve them in the more fun aspects of the wedding. Let them think they are choosing their task and are integral to making your wedding a success. Just remember that kids can be mean. I remember being about eight years old at my Aunt Karen's wedding and I was really upset because my dress was too tight. I was in a snit all day, ruined the pictures, and told her there was "no God, just an endless pit of hell." (That must have been some hell of a tight dress!) My aunt laughs about it now but as I look back, I think I was a bit jealous. She was marrying my favorite uncle, so maybe that set me off. So try not to take it personally if his children are a little all over the place—this is an emotional experience for everybody. Just make sure that they're dressed in comfortable clothing.

Who Does That?

Now to a more difficult invite question: Does anybody really invite their exes to their weddings? I know people who do but: A. What's the point? and B. Doesn't that defeat the purpose of moving on from your old life? Perhaps if you are super well adjusted you can do these sorts of things. All I know is that every movie or television show I've seen where the ex shows up at the wedding, the bride always ends up leaving her new groom at the altar to reunite with her troubled and tormented husband. Ripping off her veil, she runs in slow motion to the man who has petty much ruined her life. And in the spirit of the day, and because love trumps all, they decide to do it all over again and say, "I do."

There are many residual feelings and having people who are strong emotional triggers at your wedding is probably not a great idea. Chances are, if you're getting married, you might be a bit of a basket case, so why muddy up the equation? Surround yourself with great team players and keep it clean and simple. Concentrate on looking forward to the man you are about to marry and not the one who sued you for mental cruelty because you wouldn't have a threesome on his fortieth.

"You're Not My Mommy!"
And Other Bonding Opportunities

Let's presume you had a successful walk down the aisle and much to your utter disbelief and wonderment you are now happily married. Your man stood by you through thick and thin and got you to the place where you could actually trust and love someone again. And unlike your therapist, he listens free of charge and does house calls. I would say you're on the verge of almost having it made! And I use cautionary language here only because you might now be picking up another title that you hadn't quite counted on: the one of "heartless, home-wrecking, seizure-inducing douche bag who preys on innocent men and children to further her cause of world domination and breaking up families," and not necessarily in that order. If you married a father, you have officially become the "evil stepmother," warts and all. And quite frankly, you've got a lot of explaining to do. Even if you weren't involved in the breaking up of the marriage and it all happened quite naturally after a reasonable amount of time post-divorce, this is a tough role to step into. Most kids like their old family and don't want a reasonable facsimile. They want the real thing. So no matter what you try to do initially, it probably won't be good enough. And since there really is no *How to Be a Stepmom Without Losing Your Life* handbook, you're left to figure it out on your own.

My advice is simple: don't even bother losing sleep over it. Try being yourself while showing his children how much you really care for their father. Let them see that you recognize this is challenging for everyone and if you can personalize the message, even better. Tell them you can relate to what they are going through, especially if your ex-husband has remarried and your children are going through the same trials and tribulations. Letting them know how all this has impacted your own family can create a whole lot of empathy and that is a very powerful bonding tool. There will be lots of time to figure out the dynamics of this new blended family. What you need to do now is make it clear you're not interested in being their new and improved "mommy figure." Make it apparent that you respect the bonds of the first family and all you are interested in is being a solid, consistent, and loving presence in this second reincarnation.

Make an effort to keep the peace between your new husband and his kids and never, ever try to compete with their mother. I'm not saying to go against your new husband's wishes or to choose sides in arguments, but rather, choose to be selfless. Make your life easier and disengage from a competition you should never win—think of yourself as a contestant who disqualifies herself from the Miss America Mom pageant due to political and ethical conflicts. You will not compete against other countries in turmoil or the swimsuit portion of the program. You are better than that.

Your new man's brood could really try to make your marital bliss a marital hell—and they could succeed. Try your hardest to genuinely respect their mother and what she has had to endure (even if you hate her guts) and be clear that you're not trying to replace her, nor do you want to. You're in their father's life—good, bad, or indifferent—and hopefully you'll be around for a while.

So how about a truce? And in time, perhaps even a friendship? It really is hard to force these things and it does take time. But that doesn't mean you have to suffer in silence, either. If you're holding up your end of the bargain and really trying to pull this "blended family" thing off, then at the very least, there has to be some basic civility. You're not a doormat for the families residual divorce anger—make that one perfectly clear.

So, if little Jimmy is in the habit of telling you to "go screw yourself" and writes you notes saying he secretly wishes that you get run over by his mom's car (twice), then calmly explain, with his father present, that this type of behavior is unacceptable. If you can achieve this measured type of inter-action—being firm but caring and not trash-talking their mom—then the possibilities are endless. The death threats could stop, little Jimmy will feel better, and your car brakes won't mysteriously go out while going down a curvy moun-tainside. Embrace your new configuration with foresight and a valid living will and you'll be just fine.

And for God's sake, as I said earlier, don't ever, ever, ever try to compete with their mother because you'll lose. And even if you happen to win in some twisted way, then what good does that do anybody? This is the biggest balancing act you will ever be required to perform and I think a very simple equation applies here: always respect your new hus-band's ex-wife in her role as the mother to their children. Do not interfere, trash-talk, or attempt to bribe or influence with purchases of small yachts or sports teams. Defer to her and, in some way, make an ally here—it will be the smartest thing you ever do.

Till Death Do Us Part—Again

It's safe to say that, at this part of the program, you're in it again—happily remarried, sharing a life with someone surrounded by various children, dogs, and detailed schedules filled with homework deadlines, work commitments, and special holidays. Who knew it was even possible twice in a lifetime, but for you, it happened. Of course, there are no guarantees in life and we know that better than anyone. As a matter of fact, statistics show that second marriages fail more than the first. It seems we tend to repeat the same mistakes, and let's face it, being married is hard work. But presumably, if you have entered this institution again without being forced, you know all that.

So what will make it different for you this time? What will it take to be with this person until you draw your last breath? Perhaps your incentive lies in the fact that you never want to have the divorce cruise experience ever again and that you will work, truly work, at your union to make sure it's the very best it can be for both of you. Second chances are just that—another shot at what you perhaps didn't get right first time round. Don't use this bonus chip as a conduit for your third shot. That could be pushing it a little. You have gone through a horrendous experience that's so not worth repeating, and hopefully with all you've learned and accomplished, you simply want to get it right. You've got yourself a life partner, so perhaps you should consider enjoying it.

And just think of the benefits! You get to have sex. Okay, this might be a tad presumptuous of me, but that usually is a benefit. Trust me, personally speaking, when it's been a really long time since you've seen the male appendage unleashed, relish and enjoy any human contact you get. It's important to be reminded at least biweekly of what a man looks like naked. Also grocery shopping, running errands, and paying utility bills is way more enjoyable when done with someone you love. Chances are, you'll even phone each other a couple of times a day. Don't you love that? Phoning a man just to say hello without the possibility of him thinking that you're stalking him or electronically tracking his whereabouts? This is romance, baby! Being actively intertwined and enmeshed in each others lives without being afraid to show how much you really care. That is "remarriage hot." And you've got it!

After being alone for a long period of time you start to appreciate the power of two. Women who have gotten remarried tell me that the first time round they might have dropped the ball on the "couple" thing. Perhaps they gave up a little bit on all the intimate aspects of their relationship, and I'm not just talking sex. They gave up on the talking, on the connecting, and the fun side of their partnerships. It became a burden rather than an asset. Of course, this can happen very easily. Two careers, kids, mortgages, bills, and baggage all can get in the way of why you presumably made this union in the first place. Think about how hard we work at our jobs, our friendships, our children, and the rewards we reap in return. Did we ever put that much energy and passion into our marriages? Maybe some of us did and some of us didn't, but regardless, now you have the opportunity to enjoy the benefits of all your hard work.

Coming from the perspective of still being a party of one, I have to tell you it's not wise to underestimate the power of your new corporate headquarters. You have an equal investor who wants the company to succeed just as much as you do. No more short-selling, fraud, or embezzling. You are now like Martha Stewart—post the insider-trading thing. You held your head high, took the hits, and came back stronger than ever. That's resilience, that's courage, and that's you.

> **"Listen, I've tried gardening, bridge, and coin collecting, and nothing excites me more about old age than hot, sweaty sex with my seventy-year-old husband. That's worth living for."**
>
> ~Miriam

Now you get to share all that you've learned and acquired with someone who clearly gets the new you. You could be that woman on the diamond commercials who keeps getting eternity bands for being such a good wife and partner. She's embraced by her hot and adoring husband as he slips one piece of hardware after another on her slim and well manicured fingers. She is wearing a fabulous camelhair coat and a charcoal gray cashmere scarf and lays her willing head on his strong and broad shoulders. The music starts up and a perfect, crystal tear rolls down her cheek and lingers on her chin as he lovingly brushes it away. Remember her? Well, guess what—that can be your second marriage.

When all is said and done, and the passion and beauty fades and the years pass, you have so much more. Long walks in the park always seem new and exciting simply because neither one of you can remember what you had for breakfast, let alone which park you're in. Becoming grandparents and getting to kick the kids out when they get too irritating because guess what—they're not yours! And the best—pretending you can't hear when your kids ask you for money. Talk about the golden years! And not to keep harping on the sex thing, but research has shown geriatric physical activity can be pretty hot.

Think about it: reduced prices on travel, movies, and your meds. Half-price buffets, free museum passes, and the accomplishment of loving someone so completely that he hangs around when you have become an old fart. Youth? Fickle and fleeting. Earning devotion and love? Priceless.

conclusion

it's time to say goodbye . . . for now

Well, we've come to the end of this particular program. From start to finish, the divorce cruise has taught us a lot, hasn't it? Things we never knew about ourselves, about others, and learning the power of wanting to actively make our lives and relationships better. Adversity has become an ally, showing us that our hope and strength rests in our choices, not our circumstances.

When we started on this journey together, things were kind of in the crapper. I don't know about you, but I was a little on edge. As a matter of fact, I look back now and wonder how I even functioned. I was the woman in the baggy jeans and torn black top wandering around the San Fernando Valley wondering where my life had gone. I would look for myself in the oddest of places—friends, family, pictures, coffee shops, but I was nowhere to be found. All I remember were endless phone calls to my lawyer, Bob, lots of paperwork, and six months after the day my ex dropped the bomb, being a divorced woman. I think I changed my socks during this period, but don't quote me.

Now, well, it's all different. And it will be for you, too, if it's not already. Like something that disappears in the rear-view mirror, so do the uglier details of your past life. It's way too hard to hold on to that much anger and pain for a prolonged period of time—that just sounds like a bad marriage to me! Hopefully, after reading this book you'll realize that you are not alone in any of this. There are lots of us out there—everywhere you look to be exact. I think if you look closely, you'll start to see some really happy, empowered women who have danced around the dark side of divorce and are more than grateful to be back.

Whether alone or partnered up, we took this experience for what it gave us and not what it took away. And when all is said and done, we stood our ground and fought for what we believed in—you can't do much more than that.

So as I finish this book, on the last day of the year to be exact, I can't help but wonder what lies ahead for me. I will celebrate New Year's Eve with my children and my parents (still together!) in my new house in California, with lots of great food and phone calls to friends around the globe. And not once will I fear the great unknown. On the contrary— bring it on! I am more than ready!

epilogue

Here I am again sitting in my living room looking out the window and wondering how I ended up in California thousands of miles away from family and old friends and feeling so, well, good. Reading back over this book, I almost don't recogonize my life—but this time it is in such a good way. And how about you? How are you doing? Have you had the opportunity to acknowledge your tenacity and focus in reclaiming your life and have you now moved forward to enjoy it? I really hope so.

For me, writing this book and revisiting my divorce experience brought out all sorts of things in me that I couldn't have predicted. I became happier and more confident seeing what I had gone through and what I had managed to put (mostly) behind me. I also started to have an undeniable need to finally settle into my new life as it was and embrace

it fully. And the ultimate testament to that was being a single woman who owned her own home.

So I became obsessed with property, more specifically,
property that I would own rather than rent as I had been
doing. I wasn't sure how I was going to swing it but I knew
I had to find a permanent home for my family where I would
have a vested interest in their future and, quite frankly, mine.
And with the same obsessive compulsive behavior that got
me through my divorce, I started to apply that to my home
search. Late night scanning of every obscure real estate site,
I stumbled upon foreclosures, short sales, and fire sales—I
followed them all. And then one night on the most obscure
website ever, I saw it: a 1934 Spanish-style Colonial home
on a huge lot with pool and a little guest house. It did say
the house was in my favorite Los Angeles neighborhood but
it also said it was in another state—the whole thing was very
confusing.

It turns out wthe real estate agent who listed it was a little
senile and he temporarily forgot the house's exact location.
Throw in the sign on the lawn having an incorrect phone
number and you either have a disaster waiting to happen or
a once in a lifetime opportunity for someone. For once, I got
the latter. I made an offer and before I knew it the house was
mine, conditional on financing and a home inspection.

The house passed inspection with flying colors but the
money part, not so much. The sweat equity I put into getting my financing was almost as stressful as my divorce. I
was Canadian with no credit history here, a freelancer, and
SINGLE! I was totally undesirable to any financial institution. My mortgage broker, supposedly the best, was completely unreachable and a notorious low talker. I could never
understand what he was saying; was I approved, locked in,

locked out, or did the lender pull the plug and forget to tell me? It was like we were having the worst marriage ever—I had never felt so powerless yet so dependent on anyone. He would e-mail me at midnight and say everything was fine and then call me the next day and ask for endless documents. Once, I even went to his office and confronted him just to make sure he existed. And he yelled at me several times, even on my birthday!

My closing went way past its due date and I almost officially lost my mind. And finally when I couldn't take it anymore, I took matters into my own hands. The escrow company was waiting for my loan documents and I knew unless I did something, this painful process would drag on forever. So I tracked down the woman in charge. After being put on hold for forty-five minues, she finally answered and it all came out.

"Hi, it's Mary Jo Eustace and I know you are working very hard on my loan docs and I have heard you are a won-derful person gifted in the numerical area but unless my paperwork gets to escrow today I think my persistent stress-related diarrhea will kill me—and that would be a shame because I have been trying to buy a great new house."

Thirty minutes later I was signing my escrow papers and the deal was done. I knew I had to pull out the big guns and I did. Anytime you mention diarrhea, your request tends to get done.

The point is I learned profoudly from my divorce expe-rience that if I wanted anything done I had to do it myself, especially if it was important to me. Before my divroce, I would just hope someone would cover me but look where that got me and perhaps for you as well. Plus, where was all my fear and reluctance to just roll with life getting me?

Now I just automatically realize that it is all about embracing the inevitabilty of change and learning to love the moment without mourning its loss. And I keep reminding myself of that everyday.

Now How Is This One for a Knock-Knock Joke?

I have had a lot of surreal moments in my post-divorce life but perhaps one of the strangest happened soon after I moved back here. I got a call from a television producer, specifically a producer who was working on my ex husband's reality show. He was very polite, mentioning how great it was to talk to me and that he had heard a lot about me (yikes!) and my career in Canada. For once, I just listened intensely waiting patiently for the real intent of the phone call to come—and it did.

He was wondering how my Tuesday looked. Would I like to come by for a quick chat about, you know, perhaps being on the show? He also mentioned other career opportunities for me—and would 2 o'clock be good?

"I'll see you then," I replied.

I hung up, wondering if I was experiencing the ultimate Hollywood Moment—my big break coming in the form of portraying a broken, abandoned woman who finds redemption and self respect participating in her ex husband's reality show? Perhaps I could say that I live next door and I stalk their every move, talking directly to the camera, explaining in detail my heartbreak and mental decline as a result of all of this. Or, better still, as the producer suggested, I could have "an organic meeting where I confront Tori Spelling casually and then just express myself for two or three hours or until they say cut." We could be the perfect post-modern family, showing how everything in the long run can work out one segment at a time.

The next week, I met him at the agreed time. After I told him that I appreciated the offer to air my dirty laundry on national television, I said, "If I ever again see my son with a black X across his face on the show without my permission, we'll be having a whole different type of conversation." Then I left. Needless to say, I never heard from him again.

But you know what? The meeting was a success To this day, with huge support from family and friends, I have managed to keep my son off the reality show and cast him in the best part he could ever play—the starring role in his very own and very wonderfully private life. I mean seriously—remember the *Diff'rent Strokes* kids? Enough said.

Only Do This with a Really Close Friend

First of all, no matter how old any of us are, and how seriously we take life, isn't it important to have a little fun now and then? You know, with a good friend or a slightly deranged co-worker. Well, I happened to have both in one of my best pals, Ken, who I have known and worked with for over fifteen years. For two years we did a radio show together. Every morning at 4:30 A.M., I would see that little face, fully made up by the way, dressed head to toe in designer wear and smelling like the fragrance department at Bloomingdale's growling right back at me. Now of course we worked hard at our job but the real fun came in between breaks when we could discuss our personal lives ad nauseum. It got to the point we didn't really even listen to each other; we just sort of had two running monologues going.

During this particular time, my dating life had unexpectedly taken a positive turn and I was engaged in an almost four-week dating spurt with a man I had met online. It's all Ken and I talked about—what I should wear, the personal hygiene required (remember, there are some younger men out there who have never really seen pubic hair, thanks to the Brazilian wax) and whether smart and cheeky was better than slightly dumb and demure. Ken gave me advice on everything. Of course, some of it was completely useless (*never wear white after Labor Day, Mary Jo!*) but some I listened to. And partly because of him, I was quickly becoming a dating supernova. Until it happened: I was dumped—via e-mail.

Well we (Ken and I) were inconsolable. How could this happen? After all our hard work and dedication it was over before it really started.

Remember the section in Chapter 7 about online dating and my heartbreak over getting turfed? I told you about a spectacular payback—well, now you finally get to hear it.

This is what we came up with all by ourselves (after three weeks of brainstorming)! Motivated by my bruised ego and Ken's obsessive compulsive behavior, we devised a plan: we would create the perfect woman—in cyberspace. She would be beautiful, accomplished, well-traveled, and flexible emotionally—and let's face it, physically. Her name was Dark-HairedBeauty and she was a former lingerie model turned neurosurgeon who traveled the world doing research and fundraising. And even though she "had met some very spectacular people, all she really wanted was a down-to-earth guy who appreciated the smaller things in life." We downloaded her picture from a modeling website, gave her some good basics (36C"-24"-36") and then unleashed her into the world of online dating, specifically the site where I had met my short-term fling! She was now officially open for business.

Of course, the response was overwhelming and every-day we would check and see if my former online paramour had contacted her. For the first few days, nothing. And just when we were about to create another perfect woman, he repsonded! With the same e-mail he sent when he contacted me! Could this get any better? I flirted shamelessly with him, revealed myself one layer at a time, teased him by dis-appearing for days and then suddenly resurfacing only to go into hiding again. He was hooked. . . and so was I. I started to think that we were dating and that I had some-how morphed into DarkHairedBeauty. I even began to look to her for advice—both medical and relationship. Several times Ken had to remind me that I wasn't or never would be DarkHairedBeauty and that when our subscription to the dating site expired, so would she.

But still we persevered toward our ultimate goal—a face to face meeting between the two parties. She would be wear-ing a white trench coat, he should call ahead to the restaurant to pre-order her favorite wine, and she would be waiting at the bar. And as an added bonus, Ken would be there with a camera phone to document his face when the love of his life doesn't show up! It was like a modern love story gone awry, courtesy of the Internet.

When it came time to our meeting, the look on his face made my e-dumping well worth it. And don't worry about him—he was back online the next day, responding to our next candidate, UnderCoverWoman, a nuclear physicist who did exotic dancing on the weekend to make ends meet. I am sure they will be very happy together.

Goodbye Again

I hope after you have read this book that you can come back to it in six months or a year from now and see how far you have come. Maybe you will write your own epilogue. If you are feeling up to it, write it now, put it away, and take a look a year from now and see how far you've come. If you keep embracing this thing called change and continue to move forward I think you will be happily surprised.

So please take care of yourself in the coming months. As for me, I am just hanging with the new man in my life. He is a little demanding but very affectionate and he seems to love me no matter what I do. And I don't really mind that he chases squirrels and just ate my TV remote; he seems reliable. Now if I could just get him to stop drinking from the toilet, he would be the perfect man.

appendix

drink, drink, and be merry

When the going gets tough, the tough get drinking! And there's no tougher time to endure than when you're fighting the endless battles and heartache of a divorce. During this time some people comfort themselves with food, others can't even think about eating, but alcohol it seems, is an equal opportunity consoler. On that note, here's a recipe for a yummy cocktail that's a whole lot better to come home to than your ex ever was:

The Assho-politan

1 ounce vodka (double if you had a run in with your ex)
½ ounce triple sec
½ ounce lime juice (if you're too busy going through hell to make it
to the store, just add a few of your tears)
½ ounce cranberry juice, pomegranate juice, or your kid's juice box.
Whatever you got on hand will do just fine.

1. Fill a cocktail shaker with ice and add all the ingredients.
2. Imagine the cocktail shaker is your ex's heart and shake it as hard as you can, trying to pulverize it into a million pieces so it'll match your own heart.
3. Pour into a cold martini glass or sippy cup.
4. Enjoy slowly while stabbing pins into the voodoo doll you made from his leftover pepperoni sticks and Funyons.

Photo courtesy of www.johnwoodsphotos.com

Mary Jo Eustace

Born and raised in Toronto, Mary Jo Eustace is an author, actress, singer, chef, and mother to Jack and Lola. She graduated from McGill University with an honors degree in English and later graduated from George Brown College's culinary program.

Over the course of her fifteen-year television career, Mary Jo has been nominated for Best Host three times. After her highly publicized divorce from Dean McDermott, Mary Jo returned to her native Canada with her son and newly adopted daughter to film her cooking show, *He Said, She Said with Ken and Mary Jo* for Canada's W Network. This hit show is now in its second season.

Mary Jo is the author of the bestselling cookbook *By My Side*. She has also written for the bestselling anthology *The Other Woman* and has been featured on *Entertainment Tonight*, *Access Hollywood*, and *The Today Show*.

Today, Mary Jo lives in Los Angeles with her children.

about the Sucks Series creator

Joanne Kimes

Joanne Kimes is the creator and editor of the bestselling Sucks series. Ms. Kimes has been married for twelve years and only considers divorce during playoff season. She lives in Los Angeles with her husband and her daughter.

To find out more about Joanne and the Sucks series, please visit *www.Sucksandthecity.com*.

Printed in the United States
By Bookmasters